IT HAPPENED IN
NORTHERN
CALIFORNIA

IT HAPPENED IN

NORTHERN CALIFORNIA

Stories of Events and People That
SHAPED GOLDEN STATE HISTORY

Third Edition

ERIN H. TURNER

Globe
Pequot GUILFORD, CONNECTICUT

Globe
Pequot

An imprint of Globe Pequot, the trade division of
The Rowman & Littlefield Publishing Group, Inc.
4501 Forbes Blvd., Ste. 200
Lanham, MD 20706
www.rowman.com

Distributed by NATIONAL BOOK NETWORK

British Library Cataloguing in Publication Information available

Library of Congress Cataloging-in-Publication Data available

ISBN 978-1-4930-6028-3 (paper)
ISBN 978-1-4930-6029-0 (electronic)

♾️™ The paper used in this publication meets the minimum requirements of
American National Standard for Information Sciences—Permanence of Paper
for Printed Library Materials, ANSI/NISO Z39.48-1992

CONTENTS

ix   Preface

1   Lost in the Fog

7   A Secret Society

11   A Russian Romance

15   The Bear Flaggers Revolt

20   Patty Reed's Brave Choice

25   Gold from the American River!

30   The Head of Joaquin Murieta

34   A Soldier Resigns His Post

37   Snowshoe Thompson Delivers

39   A Winemaker's Dream

43   Jessie Benton Frémont and the Hornitos

49   Massacre on Indian Island

CONTENTS

53 Mary Ellen Pleasant Takes Her Seat

57 Emperor Norton's Decree

61 Captain Jack's Stronghold

66 An Arrest in Chinatown

70 Flames Amid the Ruins

76 Ishi

81 The Wolf House Burns

85 Silence at the Mystery House

90 The Opening of the Golden Gate Bridge

94 Statehood for Jefferson

99 The Loyalty Question

104 The Olympics Go to Squaw Valley

108 Bodega Bay Goes to *The Birds*

111 Saving a Legend Starts a Trend

115 The Summer of Love

119 They Chose Alcatraz

124 The Homebrew Computer Club

128 Christo's Running Fence

132 Harvey Milk and George Moscone Murdered

136 Harmony on Mount Shasta

140 Earthquake Stops the World Series

145 The August Complex Fire

CONTENTS

150   A Potpourri of Northern California Facts

153   Bibliography

157   Index

162   About the Author

PREFACE

Much of the early history of Northern California relates to three things: the geology, the weather, and the gold craze. Earthquakes, volcanoes, and even tsunamis have shaped the Northern California coast and its cities. Rumors of gold and other treasure spurred exploration by the Spanish and the English, then the Gold Rush brought the '49ers west. The balmy weather and excellent cropland further inland enticed settlers from the south (Mexico), from the east (the United States), and from the far northwest (Russia), while some hapless emigrants were trapped in the mountains by violent snowstorms on their way to what was touted as "the Promised Land." Amazing stories and strange characters abound in Northern California's history of exploration, domination, and the move toward civilization.

More modern stories of Northern California are also fascinating, still shaped by the geology and climate of the region, but fueled by people in search of a new treasure—personal freedom. For some groups of people, including Japanese and Chinese immigrants, former slaves heading west after the Civil War, and the LBGTQ+ community, a move to California has been a long and winding journey toward that freedom. California has been both a haven and a prison for its optimistic newcomers.

Of course, speaking of prisons, Northern California has one of the most famous in the world, "The Rock." In the twentieth century, stories of Alcatraz, the escape-proof fortress built on a former Civil War base, have entranced the world. Interestingly, it was the site, from 1969 to 1971, of a prolonged demonstration that revealed another important aspect of California's history—the relationship of newcomers to the Native Americans who inhabited the land first.

If fascinating people and issues have defined what Northern California has become, the same will certainly continue to be true in the future. For the opportunity to delve into those issues through the events described in this book, I must thank my very talented editor Megan Hiller and my uncomplaining and supremely helpful husband Ross Johnson. In addition, I have to thank my family, and particularly my dad, for long family vacations visiting the places where history happened.

1542

Lost in the Fog

The fog was so thick on all sides that the sailors believed they would never safely reach land again. Surely, they thought, they had been swept out to sea in the terrible storms of the night before, and they were halfway to China already—unless, of course, they were about to smash into unseen rocks along the coast. The rough seas on this voyage had been the worst most of the men had ever seen, and many of them thought that their commander, Juan Rodríguez Cabrillo, was foolish to have taken this assignment, and that they were even more foolish for having joined the expedition.

Cabrillo was probably wondering the same things—and thinking himself crazy—as his ship floundered on the rough waters and he struggled to see through the fog. The Spanish rightly called this coast "the northern mystery." Neither

Cabrillo nor his men could see a thing beyond the floating wooden box they called a ship! This was certainly not how Cabrillo envisioned his journey of discovery. But nothing on the entire trip had been easy or had even gone as he expected.

Back in Mexico, Cabrillo had planned for a massive voyage that would include thirteen ships of various sizes and a thousand men—including a detachment of cavalry to explore inland from the coast of the mysterious lands to the north. After the plans were set, however, his superiors had decided that an expedition to explore the uncharted territory was simply not important enough to require that many ships and men. Cabrillo was left with two ships, the *San Salvador* and the *Victoria*, both badly constructed Spanish caravels. These small, lightweight boats were not what a voyage on rough, open seas required. The ragtag assortment of rogues and drifters that were hired on as crew completed the picture of disaster that lay ahead of Cabrillo, but still he persevered in his quest to discover what of value lay to the north.

The voyage that these men had undertaken, leaving from the port of Navidad, on the Mexican coast on June 27, was daunting, and the sailors' skills were most definitely lacking, but their accomplishments had been nothing short of remarkable. In just a few months, they had traveled farther and seen more than any Europeans had yet imagined along the western coast of North America. Cabrillo claimed all of the land that he saw for Spain, stopping at various sites along the coast and declaring the will of his country with grand ceremony before his crew and the curious natives who sometimes gathered at the shore when the strange ships arrived. The local tribes thought the Spanish, with their pale skin, were ghosts and treated them with great kindness, offering them food and drink but little information about what lay to the north.

Although for the most part the expedition's luck had held out so far, as they floundered in the frigid ocean waters, trying to see through the thick fog, adding to Cabrillo's troubles was a painful broken arm. When the ships had first hit this terrible stormy weather at Point Concepcíon, they had to turn around and take shelter on an island they called San Miguel, in what is now known as Cuyler's Harbor near San Diego. It was there that Cabrillo had slipped on the rocky shore and broken his arm, which was now bandaged and almost useless. His lust for adventure was strong, however, and he insisted they continue up the coast.

Juan Rodríguez Cabrillo, or João Rodríguez Cabrilho as he was known in his native Portuguese, was an adventurer at heart, having left his village as a young man to take on hazardous duty with the Portuguese navy. He was later drawn to the service of Spain by the stories of adventure and wealth to be had in the New World, where the Spanish had a stronger foothold than any other European nation.

The native empires that had once existed in what was called the New World, or even New Spain, were being exploited by the famous conquistadors interested in their own empire building. Hernando Cortés, one of these explorers, was in the process of trying to start his own kingdom on the backs of the natives. Cabrillo joined a force of soldiers lead by Pánfilo de Narváez, who intended to end Cortés's dreams of such an empire. When Cortés defeated Narváez, Cabrillo was absorbed into Cortés's army and navy, where he gained a reputation as a fine soldier and a good leader during a war to subdue an uprising in what is now Guatemala. Cortés was eventually defeated in a later war, but many of the men who had fought with him remained in New Spain.

After the battles in Guatemala, Cabrillo married the sister of a fellow conquistador and settled down to the life of a planter in the area of New Spain known as Mexico, but wanderlust still burned in him. Cabrillo was also still recognized as a fine soldier and a leader of great energy, so when Governor Alvarado of Mexico and his partner, Viceroy Mendoza, made plans to send an expedition north up the coast of what the Spanish thought was the Island of California, in hopes of gaining further wealth and holdings for Spain in the New World, they immediately thought of Cabrillo. Cabrillo just as readily accepted the challenge.

Now Cabrillo was on the deck of a floundering ship, his arm broken, and his men in despair, but he was still determined to undertake and complete this great expedition.

In reality, when Cabrillo's men began to fear for their lives, the ships had already rounded Point Concepcíon for the second time. This time, they were not forced by the weather to turn around, but pressed on. By November 6, 1543, they had already passed the fog-shrouded bays now called Monterey and San Francisco, and on November 14, one of the ships spotted land. Before them, they could see the land on the California coast that would one day become the site of Fort Ross, about seventy-five miles north of what is now San Francisco.

Although land was finally in sight, the Spanish crews could not navigate the rough winter waters of the Pacific this far north well enough to reach the coast. After all of their effort, they had to turn around! Eventually, they drifted south to a calmer break in the coast at what is now called Drake's Bay, still north of San Francisco.

These men were the first Europeans to see the coast of northern California—but see it was all they could do. The stormy waters of the winter ocean were too difficult for them to navigate, and they were forced to turn south once again without touching down on land. They returned to the island of San Miguel, planning to spend the winter there and then return for a second try at landing on the coast they had just been so near. While they rested there, Cabrillo's injured arm became gangrenous, and he died. He was buried in an unmarked grave on the island.

Cabrillo's second-in-command, Bartolomé Ferrelo (a.k.a. Ferrer) took over the leadership of the expedition and led the ships up the coast once again. This time, the party, having left San Miguel Island on February 8, managed to make it much farther up the coast, reaching the Rogue River in present-day Oregon by March 1, 1543.

By this time, though, the men on the boats had had enough, and they forced Ferrelo to issue the command to return home to Mexico. The new captain and the wearied crew, who had now become experienced sailors, sailed back into the port of Navidad after being away for nine-and-a-half months.

In the records of the expedition, Cabrillo, Ferrelo, and their men had named at least seventy sites in northern California and reported on the general nature of the northern California coast, opening the way for possible future expeditions. However, the Spanish officials labeled the expedition unimportant because no material wealth was gained, nor did it look like any was possible. Interest in the expedition, or in any further explorations, soon faded. Much later, the Spanish would learn that the explorers had passed one of the greatest natural harbors in the world at San Francisco, and that gold lurked in the hills just off the coast—making Cabrillo's voyage of discovery one of the greatest that never came to full fruition.

1600s

A Secret Society

The children were very excited; after days of being cooped up in the musty lodge during the rains, the meeting of the secret society had finally been called. They wouldn't be allowed to go to the meeting of the society, or *kuksu*, but they would see their father and older brother painted white to look like spirits, and afterward their brother might bring another story to tell them from the wise man who held the meetings. If they were very lucky, they might even see all of the men in their white paint headed into the special earth-covered lodge where the celebration would be held. The men in the *kuksu* always looked so ghostly in the winter light, especially with the rain partially blocking the view. The children's excitement grew at the thought of seeing the leader in his feather headdress and robe.

Many of the Native American tribes of California had these secret societies, especially those in the group known as the Penutian Family. Once a year, a very important man in the Wintun tribe called a meeting of the *kuksu*, usually in winter during the rainy season. He gathered both old and young men to the meetings, where they would beat drums while he sang and danced and told stories about how the world came to be and how the Wintun were created. Telling these stories and chanting and singing was the Wintun way to pray for the well-being of their people.

The Wintun believed that animals had made the world in the beginning. They had great respect for Eagle, whom they thought was the chief world-maker, Coyote, who they called the sly one or the evil one, and who was a trickster, and all of the other animals were respected, as well. Bears were particularly important in the creation stories told by the Wintuns and other California Native Americans. They believed that Bear, who walked on hind legs like humans, was the brother of the tribes.

The Wintun were, in fact, reverent toward everything in the earth around them, not just the animals that they believed were creators of the world and of the Wintun people. They believed that the trees and the mountains had spirits, just as people did, and they were very mindful of those spirits in all of their actions.

On the night of the *kuksu*, when the men returned to their homes, the children—still wide-awake from the excitement—begged their older brother for a story from the wise man. The *kuksu* had been his first, and he was still excited, too. He wanted to tell them the story quickly so that he could remember it in the future and so that he could practice his storytelling skills. He sat with them by the warm, bright fire and told them the old tale of how the frog lost its tail.

He began: "Just after the world was created, there was no fire, and the animals were cold. The animals asked Coyote, who was known for being clever, 'Do you know where there is a fire?' Coyote answered that he thought there was fire to the north, and all of the animals went along with him to look for it.

"Soon the animals came upon a lodge with two women standing in the door and smoke coming from the roof. Coyote said, 'I will go by myself and get fire for you.' The other animals hid behind a tree near the lodge and watched as Coyote went to the door.

"Then Coyote went to the women and said, 'I am cold, and I am sleepy.' And the women invited him in to sleep by their fire. Coyote went in and pretended to sleep, and the women lay down on their skin beds and slept, too. When he was sure they were peaceful, Coyote took a burning stick from the fire and tossed it through the doorway to Panther.

"In the commotion, the women woke up and saw that Panther had the fire, and they ran to try to get it back from him. In a panic, Panther tossed the burning stick to Frog, who was the closest animal to him, but also the slowest. The women were able to grab Frog by his tail as he tried desperately to hop quickly away, but Frog managed to throw the stick of fire into the stump of a tree and then leap into a pond."

The brother ended the story, pleased that he had told it so well: "Unfortunately, Frog left his tail behind him on the bank of the pond with the women when he got away, but the fire was safe in the stump, and to this day there is fire inside any tree where whoever needs it can get it."

The children were fascinated by the story their older brother told, and that night they dreamed of animals and other stories that they might hear in time. Someday the other boys in the family would be allowed to join in the *kuksu*, and they would hear the stories and prayers of the leader and dance and chant with all of the other members. The girls could look forward to hearing the stories passed on to them by their brothers, fathers, and husbands, and be grateful that the men were praying for the well-being of all the people. As for the older brother, he dreamed of the day when he might be the wise man of the village and wear the feather robe to weave the stories of his people.

1806

A Russian Romance

Lucky for Nikolai Petrovich Rezanov, he had picked the right day to sail into San Francisco Bay from the Russian-American fur company's outpost in Alaska. The temporary commander on duty at the Presidio, the military compound at San Francisco, was Luís Antonio Argüello, the twenty-one-year-old son of the permanent military commander, José Darío Argüello. José Darío would have obeyed the Spanish injunction against foreign trade and ordered the Russian visitors to leave the bay immediately. Luís Antonio, on the other hand, was ready for some fun. He found life at the isolated Presidio boring, and here were some guests who would divert him from the stagnation of everyday life, at least for a while. The Russians, who were desperately in need of supplies, both for the continuation of their voyage and for their colony in Alaska, were certainly grateful for his boredom.

Luís went to meet Rezanov's ship himself and invited the Russians to come to his home for chocolate, a favorite drink of the Spanish, which they had discovered during their conquest of Mexico. The luckiest moment for Rezanov was still before him, however. At the Argüello home he met Luís's sister, the lovely María de la Concepcíon Argüello y Moraga, often called "Concha," for short, or "La Favorita," meaning the favorite.

Concha was a beautiful sixteen-year-old girl with straight, perfect teeth, long-lashed dark eyes, and a fine figure. She was also well educated and intelligent, certainly unequaled by any other girl in California, and head and shoulders above most of her sex in the world at that time—and even most men. Her father firmly believed that girls, as well as boys, should be educated, and he had provided her with the best his resources could offer.

In spite of her beauty and abilities, Concha had few suitors at the Presidio, because, isolated as it was, there were few eligible young men of her social class with whom she could associate. Nikolai Rezanov was forty-two years old and a widower, but still fit, and certainly charming and well mannered. He quickly fell in love with the lovely and sharp-witted Concha, and he steadily wooed her for the two weeks before her father returned to his post. By the time José Darío returned to the Presidio, the two appeared to be deeply in love.

Some historians doubt the emotional attachment between the two, or at least the attachment on Rezanov's part, because they feel that Rezanov's real motive was a stronger trade relationship with Spain in California, which he could get through the military commander's daughter. Of course, he still had a major obstacle to deal with, in the large and imposing form of José Darío and the troops in his command, before he could wed the lovely Concha and make inroads for the fur company into California.

As one might expect, José Darío was furious with his son Luís for allowing the intrusion, and with Rezanov and Concha. During José's absence, Rezanov had been hard at work gaining Concha's mother and sisters as allies in spite of their language barrier, forging trade agreements with the Franciscan monks who ran the missions, and letting it be known to the Spanish ladies at the Presidio that his ship contained trade goods such as shawls and fancy shoes. With so many adamantly supporting the couple's union, for reasons of trade if nothing else, José was forced to agree to the union, but, he insisted, Rezanov must first travel to Russia to receive permission from the Czar and to Rome to receive it from the Pope. The couple tearfully parted, and Rezanov set out on the journey to obtain the necessary permissions, which would take at least three years.

Many months passed and the lovesick Concha at the Presidio heard nothing of Rezanov, but she waited and hoped, sewing clothes for the wedding and watching as each ship sailed into the bay, hoping that one of the Russian boats she now saw regularly carried news of her beloved.

In the meantime, the Russians had taken the alliance with the Argüello family as permission to enter California and do with it what they pleased. What they pleased, of course, was to continue hunting sea otters down the coast, as they had begun doing with native Aleut hunters in Alaska in the mid-1700s. They infiltrated North America to an area just above Bodega Bay, called Rumiantzov Bay by the Russians, bringing the Aleuts with them, hoping to hunt the sea otter and to grow or trade for crops needed by the Alaskan outposts. In 1812, they set up their first permanent settlement near Bodega Bay called Fuerte de los Rusos by the Spanish, Rossiya by the Russians, and Fort Ross by the Americans, who came to know it as well. Eighty Aleuts and ninety-five Russians occupied the fort.

As for Concha and Rezanov, his luck finally ran out. As he was crossing Siberia on his way to ask for the Czar's permission to marry, Rezanov, already dreadfully ill with malaria, fell from his horse and was killed when a giant hoof crushed his head. Legend says that Concha did not hear of his fate for thirty-five years (although she probably learned the news in about ten—still a long time for a young woman in love) and when she learned of Rezanov's death, she declared her intention to never marry and entered a convent.

The Russians, however, stayed in California until 1841, when the demand for sea otter pelts and the sea otter population itself began to shrink. Then it was deemed that the cost of the outpost in California was too great and the Czar insisted that they sell it off. That they did, to a man named John Sutter, on whose land gold would eventually be found that would set off the gold rush of 1849.

1846

The Bear Flaggers Revolt

William Todd proudly unfurled his finished product and stepped back to receive the exclamations of joy from his companions. The men gathered around the table to see the results of Todd's work and exclaimed, laughing, that he must have made some kind of mistake. They wanted a grizzly bear on their flag, a symbol of their fierce, independent pride—not a common pig from a farmyard. Todd took their comments and guffaws good-naturedly. He knew he was not the greatest artist in the world, and he felt he had done his best. After all, it did not really matter that Todd's bear looked like a pig; the spirits of all the men were too high on this glorious night to dwell on the artwork for long. At last, Alta California was on the road to independence from Mexico!

By June 1846, many Americans had come west to settle the area around Sonoma, California, in what was then Mexican territory. Many of these people had been inspired to start homesteads and ranches in the area by the writings of John C. Frémont. Frémont was an Army officer who had become famous as a route finder in the West when he was commissioned to explore a route through the Rocky Mountains for settlers moving to Oregon Territory. Not content to abandon his explorations and return to the United States once he had arrived in Oregon, Frémont had traveled south into what was then called Alta California. The books he and his wife, Jessie, had written about his experiences on his expeditions had much to say about the wonderful land and opportunities in the West. People in the East were reading the books and heading for California in droves to find the promised land of plenty.

For the most part, those who had ventured west to California on Frémont's word had prospered, but the Mexican government was not pleased to have these *Americanos* living in Mexican territory while remaining citizens of the United States. Finally, Colonel José Castro, California's military commander, who was headquartered in Monterey, proclaimed that Americans had no right to the property they held in Mexican territory. In fact, he said they could no longer worship God as they pleased. Any Americano living on Mexican soil would have to become a Mexican citizen and convert to Catholicism. Otherwise, they would be expelled from their homesteads and sent back to the United States.

The Americans living near Sonoma, California, were not willing to give up all of their hard work or the beautiful country in which they had settled, nor were they willing to give up their freedom. John Frémont, who had moved to California permanently himself, had organized a small troop of men to try to form an independent government in San Francisco. Another group of men who called themselves the *Osos*, which is Spanish for bears, met and elected a leader, William B. Ide, to lead them in an attempt to overthrow the Mexican government in Sonoma.

On the evening of June 14, 1846, the Osos snuck into Sonoma, they thought unexpectedly, planning to march on the house of General Mariano Vallejo. Vallejo had already heard that the men were coming and his wife—fearing for his life—tried to convince him to flee the town, leaving her behind, as she was unable to travel. Vallejo stubbornly refused to leave her, and they were both at their house, called La Casa Grande, waiting for the Osos when they arrived.

To the great surprise of the Americans, when the rowdy bunch arrived at the house, the general invited the leaders in, peacefully surrendered when he was placed under arrest, and offered them the finest wines and spirits that his collection had to offer. Vallejo knew that he could not hold off this determined group, especially if they were soon to be joined by reinforcements, but he thought that wine and quiet negotiations would win him some time and support. However soothing the general's words and whiskey were, the men outside grew impatient waiting for their leaders and charged into the house, making demands and helping themselves to the wine and spirits.

After having consumed much *aguardiente*, as the Mexicans called strong liquor, at the general's home, the Osos decided that they must have a flag to raise over the city when they proclaimed their victory. William Todd was given the job of sewing the flag from remnants of material that were to be found in the town and painting the final design.

Todd set to work with a torn red petticoat and a piece of unbleached muslin. Based on these materials, the Osos decided that the flag should have a red stripe along the bottom border. It should also have a red star, reminiscent of the one on the flag of the Republic of Texas, which had become a part of the United States in December 1845, in the upper left-hand corner. To represent the fighting spirit of the Osos, they wanted a grizzly bear, on all fours, in the middle of the flag, facing the star.

William Todd's sewing skills were more than adequate for the job, but his painting left something to be desired. The men may have abused his drawing, claiming the finished product—rendered in blackberry juice—looked more like a pig than a ferocious grizzly, but all admitted being unable to do any better. Early on the morning of June 15, the men who were responsible for its creation raised the Bear Flag in a solemn ceremony over Sonoma, California.

Before what is now called the Bear Flag Revolt had even started, in May 1846, President James K. Polk, an expansionist, someone who believed that the United States should occupy more territory on the American continents, had made an offer to Mexico to buy California. The offer was refused, and it looked like the two nations were dangerously close to war. With the raising of the Bear Flag over Sonoma, the men declared that California was an independent republic with no formal ties to either nation, but the United States had other ideas about the rightful ownership of California, and they viewed the Bear Flag Revolt as a step toward waging war against Mexico for the permanent control of the territory.

On July 7, 1846, Commander John C. Sloat of the United States Navy ordered the United States flag raised over Monterey and officially claimed California as a part of the United States. The United States was now at war with Mexico.

In the middle of June 1846, California was an independent republic, and by the middle of July it was a contested territory of the United States. The Army marched through California and fought the Mexican army in a war that lasted nearly two years. Finally, Mexico surrendered, and on February 2, 1848, California was officially ceded to the United States.

Barely a month before, a man named James Marshall had discovered gold near what is now the capital city of Sacramento. Thousands of would-be millionaires inundated the area in the race for gold, and on September 9, 1850, California, which now had a large enough population, was officially admitted as the 31st state. The legacy of the Bear Flaggers lives on in the State of California. The state adopted and proudly flies the bear flag, first designed at Sonoma by the Osos.

1847

Patty Reed's Brave Choice

Mrs. Reed was determined. Her family had been trapped in a tiny cabin by Truckee Lake, high in the Sierra Nevada for five months, and they were starving to death. The only thing they had left to eat was a tough, leathery hide from a cow that had been slaughtered weeks ago, and its ownership was in dispute. Mrs. Graves would not let the hide, currently being used as part of the roof, be taken off her own cabin. Worse, Mrs. Reed had not seen her husband since that fateful day in the Great Basin, when he stabbed a man—in self-defense —and was banished from their wagon train.

For months, relief parties had been trying to reach the group of pioneers stuck in their wintry quarters in the mountains, but the weather was always against them. No horses could travel through the deep snow on the mountains, and it took weeks for men on snowshoes to reach the encamped party. Once the relief reached them, they usually had barely enough food to offer a scant meal to those surviving in the few pitiful shelters near Truckee Lake. When relief arrived, they would have to turn around immediately, pulling the poor, starving inhabitants who were strong enough to make the dangerous trip after them.

When a rescue party reached them in early February 1847, Mrs. Reed gathered together her family and prepared to take them out into the snow and over the mountains to where, she hoped, but hardly dared believe, her husband would be waiting. The last few months had been the most terrible, hideous experience of her life. Her children barely had enough clothes left to cover them and she despaired of their ability to climb over the deep snow in their weakened condition from so many weeks without food.

The Reeds hardly looked like the same family who had started from Missouri so many months ago in a wagon called the Pioneer Palace. Then they had traveled in style and comfort in the amazing two-story vehicle, which contained more goods and food than they could imagine in their present state—most of which had been abandoned on the trail as their situation grew desperate after Mr. Reed's exile. The oldest daughter, Virginia, probably ached with thoughts of the wonderful pony that she had ridden over so many miles before they had reached the scorching hot and dangerous desert, which had been but an evil prelude to the treacherous mountains.

After spending nearly four months trapped by heavy snows, the family started out after the rescue party, with the smallest children, Martha, called Patty, and Tommy coming behind the others, stepping in the tracks made by the snow-shoers. Patty was only eight years old; Tommy was three. Their little legs strained with the effort of following the tracks. Soon, it became obvious even to Mrs. Reed, who was determined to keep her family together, that these two smallest could not easily keep up with the group.

Patty might have been able to make it out, moving slowly behind the line, but she was very tired and would need help. The men with the rescue were already strained almost to the limit of their strength, and they knew they would not be able to carry her very much on the long journey down the western slope to safety in the valley. But even if Patty could make it, walking partway, Tommy could not, and he was too young to stay alone in the camp. He needed the care of his older sister.

Mrs. Reed became resigned to the choice she knew she had to make, but before she could speak to send them back to the camp, she looked at her little ones wistfully. Then Patty spoke her worst fears:

"Well, Mama, kiss me goodbye. I shall not see you again."

Mrs. Reed argued with the little girl, but Patty would not be shaken. She promised to take good care of Tommy and then said, "I will die willingly, if I can believe that you will live to see Papa."

The parting of the family was tearful, and no doubt Mrs. Reed was forced to believe her daughter's words. The children had nothing to eat and no promise of a rescue coming soon. She hoped that the other families still at the camp would provide for the children, but they all had children of their own, and nothing to share.

The rescue party led the rest of the Reed family down out of the mountains through the deep snow, and Mrs. Reed thought despairingly of her littlest ones back at the camp. The trip took days, and they grew weaker and weaker during the forced march through the bitter cold and snow. Surely, Mrs. Reed thought, she had made the right decision. Better that Tommy and Patty had not endured this hardship.

As they neared the end of their journey, a shout rose up. Another rescue party was coming to meet them. The snowshoers were ecstatic, but when Mrs. Reed found out who was leading the party, she collapsed into the snow, overcome with emotion. Her husband, whom she had not seen for more than five months, was leading the group that was coming into the mountains.

After making sure his wife and the rest of the children were in capable hands and well on their way to safety, Mr. Reed hurried into the mountains to find Tommy and Patty. The deep snows and rugged terrain meant that he did not reach them until March 1, and he feared the worst. To his great joy, however, they were still alive, though very weak, when he arrived.

It would be a harrowing trip out of the mountains for Mr. Reed and his two small children, but they were together at last, and soon they would be safe. As they left the little camp by Truckee Lake, Patty showed her father the most precious possessions she had in the world, two things that she had saved during their entire trip and all during that horrible winter: a tiny, beloved doll and a lock of her grandmother's hair.

Patty, Tommy, and all of the Reeds made it out of the mountains during the winter of 1847, but more of their party, the Donner Party, were not spared. Of the eighty-two emigrants who entered the mountains in October, only forty-seven would survive. Forty-two emigrants and would-be rescuers lost their lives to the harsh conditions and starvation. Some of the survivors were even forced to resort to cannibalism, feeding on the flesh from dead human bodies. Patty Reed—and all of the Reed family—would live to tell their stories, and Patty kept her doll and precious lock of hair all her life.

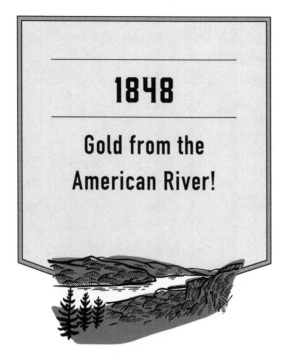

1848

Gold from the American River!

On the morning of January 24, 1848, James Marshall quietly reported to work at the site of the new sawmill that had been built on the site he had chosen on the South Fork of the American River. A new arrival to California, Marshall, who was a sober man from New Jersey, had been assigned to choose the site of the mill and supervise its building by John Sutter, a German who had come to what was then Mexican California by way of Switzerland. Having gone bankrupt in his adopted country, Sutter determined that California was the Promised Land, and he headed there intending to start a utopian empire for himself called Nueva Helvetia or New Helvetia.

On his way to California, Sutter had stopped for a time in Hawaii, and it was rumored that he brought several Hawaiian women with him to his new home as concubines. It was certainly not a rumor that he had many Indians working for him at his new location and that they were kept in a state of semi-slavery.

Luckily for Sutter, when he arrived in California in 1839, a colony of Russians at Fort Ross near Bodega Bay had just been given orders from the Czar that they were to sell off their holdings and abandon their colony. They offered their goods to Sutter for thirty thousand dollars, and he accepted the offer, on the condition that he could pay it off over a long period. When the deal was struck, he built Sutter's Fort at the confluence of the American and Sacramento Rivers, to be the center of his empire.

Sutter had become quite successful with his method of empire building, and especially with his trading post at a site forty-five miles from the sawmill, which traded with the many emigrants who were coming to California from the United States. Encouraged by the influx of settlers from the United States and seeing economic opportunity at every turn, Sutter decided to enter the lumber business, and he hired Marshall to help him do it. Variously described as brooding and eccentric, Marshall actually enjoyed his work very much and was delighted with the progress that had been made on the sawmill by his crew of Native Americans, Mormon veterans of the recent war between the United States and Mexico, and a family of settlers named Wimmer.

Marshall was not one to share his excitement, but he might have conveyed his disappointment in early January 1848, when the machinery was about to be installed in the mill and they discovered that the lower end of the tailrace that turned the main water wheel was not deep enough. Marshall ordered the men to blast out the section of river, making a deeper channel for the water to travel through.

When he arrived at the site on the morning of January 24, Marshall was again pleased with the progress that had been made. He stepped down the bank to look at the deeper tailrace made by the blast and admired the work that had been done. Then he spotted a few shiny particles—of what, he wasn't sure—in the water.

The men were curious about the particles, but not too impressed. Marshall was cautious about making too much of the find before he knew for sure what it was. He gathered the pieces and set off for Sutter's Fort and the trading post to discuss the matter with his employer.

Once back at Sutter's Fort, Sutter and Marshall devised every test they could think of to determine if the samples were actually what Marshall suspected they were—gold. Eventually, they concluded that while the pieces seemed to be genuine, the find at Coloma was probably not a large one. Even so, they agreed, it would be best to officially obtain title to the land where the gold was found, and an employee was dispatched to procure the necessary paperwork from the military governor at Monterey.

Marshall returned to the mill with his news, but the men seemingly remained unimpressed; only a few spent their spare time panning in the water, hoping for another find. When the work on the mill was complete, however, most of the workers remained in the area to be joined by friends with whom they had shared the news of the gold discovery. A few more samples were found, but the men remained calm, quiet, and satisfied to keep the news to themselves. One of the most important events in California's history had just happened in the water at their feet, but it would take some time for the world to find out about it.

The employee who had been sent to obtain the land grant at Monterey was sworn to secrecy about the find, but when he reached the village of Benecia, where the population was excited about the discovery of coal at Mount Diablo, he felt he had to share his even more exciting news. At San Francisco, the employee even showed his sample to an experienced gold miner, but still everyone he met remained relatively unimpressed.

In March, two San Francisco newspapers ran stories about the gold discovery, and Sutter himself was interviewed—but he continued to downplay the importance of the discovery. In the meantime, just a few hundred prospectors had come into the area, and Sutter was making a fairly good living trading with them. He had no real need to hope for an expansion of the find, but he also dabbled in the mining business, employing Native Americans to do the digging for him. Life at Sutter's Fort and in California remained relatively unchanged.

Then, almost in an instant, it would never be the same again. On about May 12, a man named Sam Brannan, a prominent merchant in Sutter's New Helvetia colony who was interested in increasing his own business, ran frantically through the streets of San Francisco with a bottle full of gold dust, yelling, "Gold! Gold! Gold from the American River!" Apparently the fervent cry of the man and his rapid pace finally excited the town's interest. By June 1, three-fourths of the population of San Francisco had left for Sutter's Fort. San Jose was practically deserted as well, and towns up and down the coast, as far south as Santa Barbara and Los Angeles, emptied as well.

But the biggest rush was yet to come. In his State-of-the-Union Address in December 1848, President James K. Polk announced the discovery, and the news of the strike was officially out. Soon the news had spread around the globe, and in 1849 the rush for gold in California was officially on!

James Marshall never made much money from the gold he discovered in the American River—he sold his interest in the mill for $2,000, then boasted that he knew of even richer deposits elsewhere. The miners who heard this announcement at the mill threatened to hang him unless he shared the location of the other cache. He managed to escape, but the mob tore the mill to bits.

Marshall's employer, John Sutter, was given credit for the discovery by the government and even received a pension because of it. Sutter's dreams of a utopian New Helvetia and massive wealth were ended by the Gold Rush, however. His fields were overrun by the mobs of miners who came to the area, ending his plans for an agricultural empire, and he was unable to find any workers to run the businesses at the fort. Everyone, it seemed, had gold fever—and both Sutter, ever the opportunist, and Marshall, the discoverer, were unable to profit from it. Even Sutter's scheme to use Native American miners and keep the lion's share of the profits for himself eventually failed. It was ironic that this man who had so encouraged and hoped for emigration had been ruined by it. His legacy lives on in California, however; the little fort he started did grow into a fine city, and it is now the capital of California, Sacramento.

1852

The Head of Joaquin Murieta

A large crowd gathered outside the sheriff's office that hot, dusty afternoon in the small town of Stockton, California. The office had just received word from the state legislature that a reward was being offered for the capture of the notorious outlaw, Joaquin Murieta. The sign a deputy was now hanging on a tree bearing the words DEAD OR ALIVE offered a reward in the amount of five thousand dollars for the capture of the outlaw.

Suddenly, the crowd parted and a rough-looking stranger with a prominent pistol at his side elbowed his way through. He brazenly strode up to the tree, took a pencil from his pocket, and carefully lettered, "I will pay $1,000 myself. J. Murieta." No one in the shocked crowd stopped the outlaw, who simply mounted his waiting horse and rode out of town again.

In the lawless early days of California, Joaquin Murieta was an outlaw legend. Many considered him a modern-day Robin Hood, who shared his takings with fellow Latin Americans who were persecuted in California in the years following the Mexican-American War. In the war, the United States had acquired the land that became the State of California from Mexico, and many emigrants who had come to the new state from the eastern United States were in favor of denying the rights of citizenship to Latin American residents, even if they had been there first. As a result, many Latin Americans were forced off their land by the whites.

Joaquin Murieta had a mighty rage against the *gringos*, or white Americans, who were taking over northern California. He was not completely unjustified in his anger, nor was he alone in his feelings.

Murieta had been born in Sonora, Mexico, and had drifted north to California with a circus as a young man with his wife Rosita. A brother of Murieta's joined them later, and the two of them staked a rich claim in Stanislaus County during the gold rush. Successful and happy in their new life in California, the brothers became the unwitting targets of less-successful American miners who were jealous of their success. A group of Americans beat Joaquin Murieta nearly to death, raped Rosita, and murdered his brother. Later, accused of stealing his own horse in his attempt to get away, Murieta was flogged until he collapsed from the agony.

In the years after the attack against his family, Murieta became an outlaw who traveled and marauded with his wife Rosita, who wore her hair cut short and was more than handy with a pistol. They had a sidekick, Three Finger Jack, who was also known as Manuel García. The three were among the first true stagecoach robbers in the West, and they never hesitated to murder innocent travelers or to raid settlements and camps if they thought money was to be had.

Murieta and his family were not the only Mexicans to receive ill-treatment at the hands of the *gringos*. Because of this, during their three-year career, the Murieta gang could gather up to eighty men—all of whom had been outraged, robbed, and beaten by the *gringos*—to fight the whites at a given time.

It was said that Joaquin Murieta was taking revenge on all of the men who had harmed his family. It was also said that when he did capture one of the men who had been involved, he frequently tied the man by a rope to his saddle horn and dragged him behind his horse to his death. But Murieta's fury knew no bounds; it extended even to the innocent Chinese miners in the area, whom he would capture, tie together in groups of a half-dozen or more, and slit their throats. Murieta had become a cold-blooded killer. Clearly, he had to be stopped.

Though he escaped the law many times, even on that bold day in Stockton, Murieta was eventually betrayed by a friend named William Burns, who led a posse of twenty-five men on a raid to the outlaws' camp at Tulare Lake. Three Finger Jack and Joaquin Murieta were both killed when they were awakened from a sound sleep next to a campfire by the gunshots of their attackers. The posse received the reward money, by now up to six thousand dollars.

Joaquin Murieta's head and Three Finger Jack's hand were removed by an opportunistic member of the posse, who proudly displayed them in San Francisco preserved in a jar of whiskey. He shared his treasure with the curious in San

Francisco for the admission price of one dollar. The head was regarded almost as a religious icon by some superstitious Mexican supporters of Murieta's crusade. Some of the more superstitious among them claimed that it even continued to grow hair.

Many people, including Rosita, Murieta's long-suffering wife and partner, declared that the head was not his at all. She claimed that Murieta had escaped to Mexico with a herd of horses and fifty thousand dollars, and other friends of his in northern California would testify to seeing him alive years after his supposed capture and death.

His head, whether real or a hoax, wasn't the only thing that remained of Murieta in California. He was the stuff of legend, and the stories of his deeds still abound today. In fact, almost all of the stories about Joaquin Murieta are just that, legend, including the story of his bold strides into Stockton. There were a number of outlaws in California at the time Murieta was supposed to have been terrorizing settlers and stagecoach drivers who also took credit for his deeds, and no one really knows who was responsible for all of them.

1854

A Soldier Resigns His Post

On February 2, 1854, a young soldier stationed at Fort Humboldt wrote to his wife in Missouri, "You do not know how forsaken I feel here." A few days later, he wrote, "I could almost [quit and] go home 'nolens volens.'" A month later he wrote, "I sometimes get so anxious to see you and our little boys, that I am almost tempted to resign and return to Providence, and my own exertions, for a living where I can have you and them with me."

Indeed, the last two years had been almost unbearable for the young captain, who was now deeply depressed. He had been in the Army since his graduation from West Point and had served valiantly in the Mexican War, but this was the first time since their marriage in 1848 that he had been away from his also-young wife and their two tiny children. In fact, he had never even seen his youngest son, who was born after he left for his post in California.

The soldier had left his wife in Sackets Harbor, New York, in 1852 at the fort on the shore of Lake Ontario, precisely because of her delicate condition. The soldier would have to cross the Isthmus of Panama to get to California, and it was a dangerous trip even for people in the best of health. In fact, about a third of the people in the group he crossed with would become sick and die before reaching the golden coast.

In addition to worries about his wife, the young soldier had other concerns on his mind when he headed west. During the Mexican War while he was quartermaster for a regiment, a large sum of money, one thousand dollars, had been stolen. He was never able to prove who had taken the money, and it was his responsibility as quartermaster to pay it back. One of his goals on arriving in California would be to make enough money to pay his debts. The other would be to make enough money to provide a pleasant home for his wife and their two young children when they could finally travel and join him there.

Almost as soon as he had arrived in San Francisco, he wrote to his wife, "There is no reason why an active energetic person should not make a fortune every year." Unfortunately, all of the moneymaking schemes he tried failed, either because he was too trusting in a friend, or because the weather destroyed his crops when he tried farming near his post at Fort Vancouver in Oregon Territory.

But through all of the business ventures, he still missed his wife and family terribly, and it clouded all of his efforts. In 1854 when he was transferred to tiny and bleak Fort

Humboldt on the California coast, he was broke, exhausted from the labor of trying to make a living in addition to his Army pay, and drinking heavily. In addition, he had no hope of seeing his wife and sons soon, as he couldn't afford to send for them. Even if they could make the journey, once in California he wouldn't be able to provide a servant, or even a decent house, for his wife, and he couldn't bear the thought of her and the children suffering with him on the wild frontier.

The depressed man did everything he could to try to get a transfer to a post closer to home, but his commanding officer wouldn't hear of it, and the young soldier slipped further into his loneliness. Formerly outgoing and gregarious, he stayed alone in his room much of the time and was seen drinking heavily on more than one occasion, which led to wild rumors about his instability as an officer.

Eventually, he was forced to give up. In April 1854, he submitted his letter of resignation from the Army, to be effective on July 31, 1854. He spent the next two months finding his way home by begging and borrowing, as he had no money to pay for standard transportation.

In October 1854, the soldier, whose name was Ulysses S. Grant, was reunited with his beloved wife and children. For the next several years he lived with them and worked as a civilian, but his Army career was not officially over. When the Civil War broke out in 1861, Grant was called back into active service, and he would become beloved as the general who won the war for the Union. In 1868, the once-lonely soldier and now world-famous general was elected the president of the United States.

1856

Snowshoe Thompson Delivers

The residents of Placerville, California, couldn't believe what they were seeing. "Snowshoe" Thompson, a young immigrant from Norway, had just strapped two ridiculous-looking boards to his feet and was gliding over the snow toward them with an eighty-pound mail sack strapped to his back. On these narrow boards, he claimed, he could carry the mail to and from Genoa, Nevada, and keep the snowbound residents informed of outside affairs during the long, cold winter.

The skis, or "snowskates" as the locals called them, that Thompson crafted out of sturdy valley oak were ten feet long, with an eight-inch upward curve at the toe. They tapered from a width of six inches at the toe to four inches at the heel, and they were two inches thick at the toe strap, which served as the only binding. All told, they weighed twenty-five pounds.

On these simple wooden boards, Thompson carried the mail for fifteen winters. On his first trip, Thompson made it from Placerville to Genoa in only four days, and eventually he would reduce the time it took to make the 110-mile journey to three days eastbound and two days west, where the downward slope of the Sierra made for a pleasant, if not frighteningly speedy, glide. He always went alone and carried with him only dried beef and hard biscuits. His mail service was the only way the snowbound Placerville could communicate with family and friends, or conduct business in the outside world through the hard, cold winter.

In the 1850s, California's first organized ski races were held at La Porte (Rabbit Creek) and skis were not an uncommon means of transportation, but few had taken them to the edge of their usefulness quite like Thompson. The skiers at La Porte were known for their speed, and in 1860 they opened their ski races to outsiders. Snowshoe Thompson was invited, but it is said that he lost his backers' $500 when he failed to win the race.

Still, Thompson's case may have proved that the race goes neither to the swift nor to the persistent. During all the years he carried the mail over the treacherous mountain route, Thompson never charged for his services. He had been hired by a postmaster who actually had no authority to hire and no payroll to back up his decision, and so the appropriate government compensation never found its way into Thompson's pocket. In spite of the fact that he never failed in his duty, bringing the mail through worse than sleet, snow, and dead of night, he was never compensated for his years of service to the people of Placerville. He died on May 15, 1876, after years of petitioning the government for his back pay.

1858

A Winemaker's Dream

The visitors to Count Agoston Haraszthy's new California estate were amazed. The Hungarian had been in the Sonoma Valley only a short time—and it was rumored that his new business wasn't going quite as well as he had hoped, yet. But here they were, standing in front of his beautiful chateau, overlooking the vineyards of his fledgling winery. He had been right after all; the California soil and climate were perfect for growing grapes. And it was certainly true that the men who were still seeking gold in the California hills and the merchants who had come to supply them were thirsty.

Count Haraszthy wasn't the first man to grow grapes for wine in California or even in the Sonoma Valley. The first man who had done so in the Sonoma Valley was Franciscan

Friar José Altimira because he needed sacramental wine for his mission, Mission San Francisco Solano, in 1824. His was a small winery, closed when the mission was no longer used, but he had noted the ease of growing the grapes in the region and had compared the results of his small operation to the finest wine of Europe.

However, mostly because of the lack of transportation to major markets and the lack of a market in California, the wine-making potential of the valley had not yet been tapped when Count Haraszthy had the idea to start his winery. Traditionally, wine came from regions where river transportation was nearby, and the Rhine, Rhône, and Loire river valleys of Europe had become famous for the quality of their wines because of the ability of the vintners to transport it so easily. In California, the area around Los Angeles was already being extensively used for grape growing and wine production. In 1858 alone, Los Angeles County had produced 500,000 gallons of wine; now all the growers there needed was a way to reach the world.

The Sonoma Valley's climate and growing season were similar to the famous European grape-growing regions, but transportation would still be a problem for Haraszthy, just as it was for vintners in Los Angeles. However, Count Haraszthy wasn't one to let anything stop him. He tried everything to get his winery going, lobbying the legislature for funding and trying to interest other settlers in growing grapes and forming a cooperative organization. In 1861 he was authorized by the California legislature to make a trip to Europe to bring back grapevines of different varieties for growing in the California soil. Haraszthy paid for the trip himself when the legislature provided authorization, but no funding.

Haraszthy had named his new winery Buena Vista for the beautiful view that he had from his vineyards—the place was the picture of a country gentleman's estate. The grapes he planted in this lovely setting were Rieslings, Pinots, Zinfandels, and Tokays, all of which he brought with him from Europe. His operation was small at first. Although he had just a small building for processing the grapes, he had big plans. He would eventually build his own pressroom and have a large cave dug out of the side of a hill where he could ferment the wine in oak barrels. Still, he couldn't share his products with the world, as he would have liked.

Others in the area joined in the winery business, as well, and Haraszthy formed the Buena Vista Vinicultural Society in 1863 as a result. These vintners planted other varieties of grapes, and a thriving agricultural industry was born. Then, in 1869, a massive change occurred that meant the wine business would be highly profitable for those who tried it in the Sonoma Valley. The first transcontinental railroad was completed at Promontory Summit, Utah. This connected the city of Sacramento, California, with the East Coast at a speed that was never possible before, opening up new markets for the wine in the East.

The impact of the transcontinental railroad on the world of wine was enormous. From Haraszthy's small winery, a massive industry grew that changed the way wine was viewed all over the world. For one thing, California wines came to be named for the grape they were made from, whereas in Europe, the wines were named for the region in which they grew. Second, suddenly the European wines had competition in the American market, from a homegrown product. Eventually, in the Sonoma Valley alone, more than 13,000 acres of vines would be planted, producing 300,000 cases of wine per year. In fact more than 350 million gallons of wine are made in California each year.

As for Count Haraszthy, he probably wasn't a real count—he just adopted the title because he thought the effect was good. His impressive French chateau on the vineyard site may not have been a real chateau, either. In the earliest days of the winery, when the fields were full of grapes, but no wine had yet been produced, Haraszthy set out to build an impressive chateau thinking that the only thing his new vineyard needed was an impressive home for the vintner. The legend says that, unfortunately, he soon realized that after all of his other expenditures, he didn't have the money to do the whole thing. Instead, he built just the grand façade, like a movie set, and then he propped it up from behind with timbers. An artist's rendering of the façade became the Buena Vista label, but the grand chateau never existed during Haraszthy's lifetime. The Buena Vista winery, however, still exists today, and its original pressroom has been revamped as a tasting room. Haraszthy would be proud to see the results of his labor. Unfortunately, he was unable to see much of his work come to fruition. He lost most of his holdings in 1866 and headed south to Nicaragua where he drowned in 1869.

1858

Jessie Benton Frémont
and the Hornitos

The color drained from Jessie Benton Frémont's face as she read the message that had just been handed to her by the boy seated on the horse. The note said that unless she abandoned her home within twenty-four hours, it would be burned and her husband would be killed.

Then Jessie's eyes blazed and she bravely snapped at the messenger, "No answer." But as the messenger rode away, her knees buckled with fear. If she left her house now, she might lose it forever; and she had come too far to lose it to a band of ruffians and an unjust law.

Jessie was the daughter of the famous senator from Missouri, Thomas Hart Benton, and nothing in her upbringing should have led her to a life on a ranch in the new state of California. Her mother was a southern belle from Virginia, and as a young belle herself, Jessie had caught the eye of an adventurous young soldier named John Frémont. The two began a secret romance when Jessie was only sixteen and the dashing Lieutenant Frémont was twenty-seven. Jessie's family disapproved of the match and did everything they could to keep them apart; her father even had Lieutenant Frémont named the leader of several frontier expeditions, hoping that either he would fail to return or the time spent apart would change his daughter's mind.

After Lieutenant Frémont returned from one of his adventures to the West, however, the young coupled eloped against Jessie's family's wishes. Jessie was Frémont's partner in his adventures from that moment on.

Ironically, the effort that Senator Benton put into keeping his son-in-law away from his daughter made John Frémont a famous man, and Jessie's assistance would help make him more famous, yet. Early in their marriage, Frémont would go on his expeditions and then return to have Jessie help him write his reports. After several years of spending so much time apart, however, Jessie made the long trip from Missouri to northern California to live on her husband's ranch, called the Mariposas. The ranch was on a very valuable piece of land—gold had been found there!

At first, life at the Mariposas was wonderful. Although there was not a house big enough on the land to hold the Frémonts' family, Jessie arranged to have several small log buildings moved together, then connected by a long veranda. As a crowning touch, she had the entire structure whitewashed, and it became known locally as the White House. Inside, Jessie placed the finest furnishings to be found in California at the time. As the wife of a famous explorer and the owner of a gold mine, she could afford the best. French wallpaper, fine carpets, and beautiful silk draperies filled the house. She even had a piano delivered from San Francisco. When it arrived, she and the local blacksmith tuned it. He would turn the pegs while she listened to the notes and she would cry, "Stop!" when the sound was correct. The house was beautiful, inside and out, and it would break her heart to have to leave it.

When Jessie squared her shoulders and sent the messenger away, she already had a plan. She knew trouble was coming. Late the night before, a man with a worried-sounding voice had called her husband from the house. Frémont had tried to reassure her that it was just mining business, but Jessie knew better.

Chief Justice Terry of the California Supreme Court had recently ruled that any mine that was left unattended, even temporarily, was free for the taking. As a result, mine owners started keeping workers busy in their mines twenty-four hours a day to protect them from claim jumpers. A group of men called the Hornitos who had no land had decided to take advantage of the law. They organized a league to drive out the mine owners and take their claims for themselves.

The Hornitos had bribed the workers at one of Frémont's mines and convinced them to leave, then claimed the mine for themselves. A few of them stayed behind to fend off thugs with similar ideas, and the rest moved on to an adjacent mine, the Josephine, planning to do the same thing. When the Hornitos arrived at the Josephine, they set up camp, but could not be in legal possession of the mine because there were still a few workers busy deep inside. In an effort to get the remaining miners to leave they set up barricades on all of the roads going in or coming out. They planned to keep supplies from reaching the miners, and after starving them out, the mine would be theirs.

John Frémont knew that the Hornitos were after his mines, and he left late in the night to confront them. Jessie had already made plans of her own when the messenger arrived at her door. She knew that somehow word had to get to the governor at Sacramento so that he would send help. Her oldest daughter, Lily, wanted to carry a message to a friendly mining camp on her favorite horse, but Jessie wouldn't allow it. Finally, it was decided that seventeen-year-old Douglass Fox, called Foxy, a boy who was staying with the family, would go.

Jessie, Lily, and Foxy carefully wrapped the feet of the horse with rags to muffle the sound of its hooves, and then Foxy set out for a friendly camp that could spare someone to send to Sacramento for help. Just after the messenger bearing the news that they must leave or be burned out left, Foxy came riding up to Jessie. He had been successful! The governor was going to hear their pleas.

Jessie knew that she had to act quickly to protect her home and family, so she told a servant to harness her horses to their finest carriage, using the fanciest livery. She then told the servant to dress himself up, too, and she put on her finest gown and got in the carriage. She wanted to look regal and ladylike when she made her stand.

At first the servant protested when Jessie told him where she wished to be driven, but she demanded that he obey her command. She wanted him to drive her to Bates Tavern in Bear Valley, the headquarters of the Hornitos. Once there, she demanded to speak to Mr. Bates.

Her stately bearing and icy tones frightened Mr. Bates. Jessie said, "What they demand is against the law. You may come and kill us—we are but women and children, and it will be easy—but you cannot kill the law."

She continued with even tones though she was terrified that she might be killed at any moment. "If the house is burned, we will camp on the land. If the men kill the colonel, we will sell the property to a corporation which will be much harder to deal with than he is." She then told Mr. Bates about Foxy's ride and the message that was to be delivered to the governor.

When Jessie had delivered her message to Mr. Bates, she told Isaac, the servant, to turn around and drive her home. She kept her calm on the seat of the wagon, even though she still expected to be shot in the back at any moment and quivers of fear were nearly shaking her from the seat. However, she arrived home safely and collapsed on a sofa in tears, shaking with sobs of terror.

Late in the night Jessie and her daughter, Lily, were awakened by the sounds of tin-can bombs exploding outside the house. But the bombs were just intended to frighten them, and though they were frightened, they still refused to leave the house. They made it through the twenty-four hours unharmed.

Several days later, the Hornitos' siege on the Josephine was broken when the miners convinced them that they would never leave the land and that the governor would back them up. Jessie had been partially responsible for convincing the Hornitos to back down. Later, the true meaning of her efforts was revealed. A group of miners' wives dressed in their finest clothes rode up to the White House to thank Jessie for not abandoning them to the Hornitos. If she had abandoned her house, there almost certainly would have been a fierce battle on the ranch land and many lives might have been lost. Her bravery in informing the Hornitos that she would not leave had saved the mines and the miners from destruction.

1860

Massacre on Indian Island

As daylight illuminated quiet Indian Island in Humboldt Bay, a grisly scene appeared amid the silent trees. Pools of blood stood on the ground near huts, and the building walls and the grass were colored red. Another look revealed the source of the blood, the murdered bodies of Wiyot Indians.

The *Northern Californian*, the weekly newspaper in Uniontown (which is now called Arcata), reported the gruesome details for its readers. "Some had their heads split in twain by axes, others beaten into jelly with clubs, others pierced or cut to pieces with bowie knives. Some struck down as they mired; others had almost reached the water when overtaken and butchered."

In the 1860s, as more settlers entered California in search of the land of plenty revealed in the gold rush of 1849, tensions had mounted between the native inhabitants of the state and the farmers and ranchers who wanted to subdivide their ancestral land into fields for crops and grazing livestock. It was only natural that California was the site of battles between the encroachers and the natives. Both Indians and whites were drawn to the bounty California's land offered, and as a result there were more Indians concentrated in what is now California in pre-European days than there were anywhere else in the United States. The California Indians had strictly observed tribal boundaries. Seldom would a Wiyot or a Karok wander from the region that had been home to their people for generations. In those regions they knew how to find the finest acorns for pounding into flour for bread or where the best fishing and hunting could be found. Unfortunately, white settlers were most interested in settling that same land where the fishing was so good, the hunting easy, and the capacity for crop growth unparalleled.

As the Indians were forced into smaller and smaller regions where the sources of food and shelter were not as good, many of them had resorted to cattle rustling and even attacking and robbing wagon trains full of settlers as they crossed California on their way to homestead and further occupy Indian land. Two groups that were especially notorious for their thievery were the Modocs and the Klamaths, tribes with territory that bordered that of the Wiyots. Soon an outcry went up from the settlers in those areas complaining of the savage Indians.

Unfortunately, most white settlers didn't distinguish between the different groups of Indians and many weren't interested in taking legal means to settle their disputes. The expression, "the only good Indian is a dead Indian" was used profusely by rugged ranch hands and matronly housewives alike. More and more skirmishes broke out between whites and Indians, and in Humboldt County someone got the idea to remove the Wiyot tribe for good.

The irony of it was that on the night before the massacre, the peaceful Wiyot people had gathered for a religious ceremony on Indian Island. As dusk had gathered on the small patch of land just off the shore in Humboldt Bay, they were gathered in prayer and made their supplications to the great spirits to see their people safely through whatever lay ahead. Then they went to sleep, grandparents, mothers, fathers, and children together.

The whites snuck quietly onto the island, just the second island out in the bay from Eureka, and let loose their fury. Almost the entire tribe was wiped out by a bunch of men with clubs, knives, and guns.

No one was ever brought to trial for the murders, and it was never publicly known who was responsible for the atrocities on Indian Island that night. There were many suspects among the citizens of Eureka who were in positions of authority in the community, and if they were in fact involved, they were able to hide their crime behind their sterling reputations and an unwillingness in the community to admit that community leaders had played a role.

Even today the healing process is still continuing in Eureka, California. In 1992, a memorial for the victims of the heinous crime began, when on February 25 a candlelight vigil was held on the island. About seventy-five people, Indian and white, attended the healing vigil and in subsequent years that number would grow to around three hundred and candles would be lit not only on the island but also in southern California, in Oregon, and on a Navajo Indian Reservation. The gathering has continued, and each year people come together on the island to work toward peace.

1866

Mary Ellen Pleasant Takes Her Seat

Clearly, the driver of Car Number 6 of the Omnibus Railroad Company in San Francisco did not know who he was dealing with. To him, the tall, stately black woman looked like just another former slave, one of many who had fled to California seeking opportunity after the Civil War, and he ordered her off the steps just as he would have done to any other black who approached his car. Perhaps he didn't notice that she was as finely dressed as any of the white women he picked up on his regular route. He probably didn't notice the anger that flashed in the woman's eyes when he ordered her off the car either, but he would certainly hear about it later.

On October 18, 1866, the front page of the *Daily Alta California* carried what could be considered a strange story for its time. Had it appeared in a newspaper in 1966, it would hardly have caused the reader to pause. The paper reported,

> Mrs. Mary E. Pleasants, a woman of color, having complained of the driver of car No. 6 of the Omnibus Railroad Company's line, for putting her off the car, appeared yesterday in the Police Court and withdrew the charge, stating as a reason for doing so that she had been informed by the agents of the Company that negroes would hearafter be allowed to ride on the car, let the effect on the Company's business be what it might.

Mary Ellen Pleasant, the woman the driver had unwittingly removed from his car, also known as Mammy Pleasant, was one of the wealthiest and most powerful women in San Francisco—even in California. She was also a hundred years ahead of the freedom riders who fought to desegregate the South in the 1950s and 1960s.

Of course, Mary Ellen Pleasant was a strange woman, strange because in her time it was unheard of for a woman to stand up to authority or to challenge society's norms by being a successful businesswoman. She was especially strange because she wasn't a white woman of privilege but a black woman with a power of her own devising.

No one knows exactly where or when Mary Pleasant was born, and the legends surrounding her past are so numerous that they may never be sorted out, but she was probably born to free parents in the segregated city of Philadelphia, Pennsylvania, on August 19, 1814. Her father may or may not have been white; some even suggested he was a southern slaveholder. Others claimed that he was a Cherokee Indian or a Kanaka—a native from Polynesia. Her mother was a black woman—presumably a former slave—from Louisiana.

As a girl, Mary was sent to Nantucket to live with a Quaker family and to be educated. Unfortunately, the Quakers kept the money that was to be used for her education and, instead, sent Mary to work. Mary Pleasant always regretted her lack of formal education, but it wasn't enough to hold her back. She left Nantucket and returned to Philadelphia when she was about fourteen or fifteen, and met and married a wealthy black man named James Henry Smith. The couple became deeply involved in the fight for abolition of slavery, and they were fervent supporters of the Underground Railroad. After they had been married for a few years, James Smith died, leaving Mary a substantial fortune. She went on to marry a former slave named John James Pleasant in 1848.

Not much else is known of either of these husbands, as it seems that Mary's life was really a one-woman show. In fact, she was known to have said of herself in later years, "I am a whole theatre to myself." She was certainly capable of taking on any role and of taking on anyone who stood in her way.

Sometime between 1848 and 1852, the Pleasants emigrated to California, following the paths of many black and white abolitionists from Philadelphia. They settled in San Francisco, and Mary, now known as Mammy Pleasant by many, made a living working as a housekeeper in the homes of several of the wealthiest merchants in San Francisco. She made several very wise investments with her first husband's fortune during these years, gleaning information about the best way to increase her fortune through careful listening during the lavish dinner parties she oversaw during her tenure as housekeeper for some of the most powerful men in

California. By 1855, she had amassed quite a sum and was the owner of several San Francisco laundries. She was also the holder of enough secrets, also gleaned from years of careful watching and listening, to make her a powerful force to be reckoned with.

This shrewd businesswoman could have been one of the wealthiest people in California if she had been interested in making money, but for her the money was but a means to an end. She built a fabulous mansion at the corner of Octavia and Bush streets in San Francisco, which was rumored to be a notorious brothel, among other things. But almost as soon as she had money from her various enterprises, she gave it away, for the most part using it to bring freedmen and fugitive slaves to California and to help them get on their feet once they arrived. Her philanthropy was extensive, and she exercised considerable political clout as well. In fact, it was probably the support of Mary Pleasant and her fortune that got a law forbidding black testimony in a court of law repealed.

Clearly the driver who tried to put her off the streetcar did not know who he was dealing with, for if he had he would have saved himself and the bus company a great deal of trouble. The people who knew her described Mary Pleasant as a formidable, terrifying woman. Others said "[If she] had been white and a man, she would have been president," and "Even as a woman she might have commanded an army successfully." She certainly proved that regardless of your sex or race you could be a success, and she used her success to help others who were less fortunate.

1872

Emperor Norton's Decree

When Emperor Norton walked into San Francisco's largest bank, or anywhere in town, people stopped and stared. He was a chubby, short man, with an unremarkable beard and mustache, and uncertain hygiene. He was frequently accompanied by two scruffy dogs, Bummer and Lazarus—and wore imperial regalia of his own devising. It was Emperor Norton's striking uniform that caused the biggest stir when he entered any bank or business. It combined the best elements of the full-dress uniforms of the American Navy and Army and was topped off by a tall beaver hat adorned with three feathers held by a golden clasp.

According to legend, with regal bearing, Norton strode through the bank and politely asked to see the president. Once an audience was granted, he presented the banker with a check for three million dollars, issued from Norton I, Emperor of the United States and Protector of Mexico, "to build a bridge over San Francisco Bay."

Joshua Abraham Norton had been born in England around 1818 and had appeared in San Francisco as a merchant in 1848, prepared to make his fortune during the gold rush of the late 1840s and early 1850s. In later years, it was said that he started his business with $40,000, earned $250,000 in the height of the rush, and then lost it all and was unable to pay his creditors. He quickly fell from his prominent position, much as many other upstart merchants had when creditors required payment they could not provide.

But, unlike the other hapless gold-rush merchants, Norton eventually rose to the top of society again, in 1859, with the air of a conquering hero bearing a royal title. The strange little man in his odd costume became beloved around town, and stories of his grand deeds and proclamations as emperor became legend. It was said that he had repaid all of his gold-rush–era debts before his disappearance, and now he paid his way about town with his own currency—printed by a friendly press in San Francisco that was sympathetic to the rather eccentric man. Tolerant and highly amused vendors and shopkeepers accepted this scrip all over the city because of the positive publicity that being one of Norton's official suppliers of provisions brought.

Many newspapers printed Norton's proclamations, some fraudulent and some from the hand of the emperor himself. It was amazing how quickly and wildly the myth surrounding the eccentric man grew. One story spread the rumor that only once was his money not accepted, by a waiter in a dining car on a train bound for the legislature in

Sacramento. According to the tale, Emperor Norton, naturally, became angry and threatened to revoke the railroad's franchise, but when the conductor discovered the error, he presented his apologies to Norton and begged a royal pardon, which was graciously granted. The Union Pacific got some great publicity from the equally fictional tales that reported Norton had received a lifetime pass to all services on the railroad.

When Norton traveled, his way was usually paid by groups that had invited him to make personal appearances. In January 1864, he went to Sacramento where he addressed the legislature and generally enjoyed the goodwill of all involved in the then-corrupt business of state politics. Norton also paid close attention to international affairs, corresponding with Queen Victoria of England, the German Kaiser, and the Tsar of all Russias. He even commanded President Abraham Lincoln to marry the widowed Victoria. Legend says that the married Lincoln's secretary responded in all due haste replying that the president would "give careful consideration to the command."

By selling "Imperial Bonds" to tourists, Norton was able to maintain his uniform and he was given "free" meals all over town (mostly in saloons that already offered free noontime meals) in exchange for his scrip. When he entered a theater, the crowd would rise to acknowledge his presence; when he met anyone on the street he expected, and usually received, a bow. In exchange, Norton strode along the wharves inspecting fruit and vegetable stands and issued visionary proclamations regarding the well-being of the city and the world. Norton ruled the world from San Francisco for nearly twenty-seven years.

Stories of Emperor Norton and his proclamations and needs became so prolific that it is hard to distinguish fact from fiction. If his check was, in fact, presented at the bank for the building of a bay bridge, it was, of course, politely accepted and acknowledged with the sincere gratitude it deserved, especially coming from the hand of the Emperor himself—but it was never cashed. Dismissed as a crazy idea from an eccentric—beloved or not—a bridge would not be built across San Francisco Bay during Norton's lifetime. The first bridge to cross a part of the San Francisco Bay was the San Francisco–Oakland Bay Bridge, which opened in 1936. Its companion in the bay—the Golden Gate Bridge—was not finished until 1937.

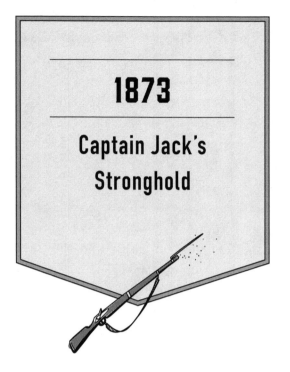

1873

Captain Jack's Stronghold

The small band of Modoc Indians had been hiding in the underground cave for weeks, and now, on the night of January 16, 1873, U.S. Army troops were approaching their stronghold, ready to force them out. The Modocs, led by Kientpoos, also known as Captain Jack, knew that they were outnumbered, that the Army's weapons were superior to their own, and that there was little chance of survival if they were forced out of their temporary home in this protective shelter in the lava beds.

While the Army was huddled beyond the rocks in the darkness, the Modocs were in their natural fortress, praying, dancing, and singing. Their shaman, called Curly Haired Doctor, had placed eight consecrated sticks around their stronghold, and a long, red cord was stretched around the stronghold as well. These were deadly to white men, he assured the frightened Modocs—mostly women, children, and the elderly. As good measure, however, he smoked his pipe and consulted with the spirits. Then Curly Haired Doctor called down a thick, low-lying fog to conceal the Modocs from their enemies.

By the time the Army marched on the lava bed fortification where the Modocs were hiding in January 1863, the war had already been more than ten years in the making. When the push to settle northern California and southern Oregon began in the late 1840s and early 1850s, the settlers began to have frequent clashes with the local Indians tribes, most notably the Klamaths and the Modocs. The 1840s had seen a number of murderous raids on whites entering the area, and as the Oregon Trail received more traffic in the 1850s, the situation worsened. The Modocs and the Klamaths were related tribes, but they became enemies during the years of difficulty between the whites and Indians, which made the land even more dangerous for whites to settle or even pass through.

Starting in the 1860s, settlers in the new state of California began protesting the thefts, murders, and livestock depredation they attributed to the Modocs and the Klamaths. In 1870, after years of treating the Klamaths and Modocs as mere nuisances, not a real threat, the U.S. government responded to the complaints by arranging to move them onto a reservation together—away from land that had been originally promised them. It was no wonder Captain Jack had decided to resist the move.

The lava beds where the Modoc were hiding were known as the Land of Burnt-Out Fires or Hell with the Fires Gone

Out. The area had seen significant volcanic activity in the ancient past, and the result of its fiery origins was an area filled with empty tube-like caves, pits, and strange formations that made the area the perfect stronghold for those who were familiar with the terrain. They could find their way out and could hold their own in battle with anyone who tried to find their way in.

The cave where Captain Jack and Curly Headed Doctor were secured with their band was nothing more than a kettle-like pit, fifteen feet in diameter at the surface, and swelling at the bottom. The sixty Modoc warriors could easily protect this stronghold, where 224 caves, 16 craters, and 75 fumaroles made the Army's approach nearly impossible. They simply didn't know the strange terrain well enough to find the Modocs and the many holes and craters made the approach slow and dangerous.

At dawn, the Army began their approach, but the fog was too thick for them to see the Modoc or to traverse the area quickly. Apparently, Curly Haired Doctor's pleas to the spirits had worked. Shortly after the Army began their attack, the Modocs returned fire. The battle waged on during the day, with heavy casualties on the side of the Army. Toward the end of the day, the fog lifted and the exhausted soldiers believed the end of the battle had come, but the Modocs surprised them from behind, trapping them in the lava beds. The Army's attack had been a complete failure, and when the battle ended, only a few soldiers returned to camp.

General Canby, the leader of the Army troops, was devastated when he learned of the Modocs' success and believed that there was no way he could force the Modocs out as he had been ordered to without losing up to a third of his forces. In addition, he really wanted to assure peace with the Modocs—he was a good friend of Captain Jack before the hostilities. Canby organized a peace commission to meet with Jack and his council in February 1873.

Jack was also ready to make peace, but he believed that peace would happen only when the soldiers were gone and the Indians were left to the land they occupied at the lava beds. Still, he agreed to meet with Canby and the others, planning to hear him out. Before the meeting, however, it became obvious that the other Modocs in the war council were not interested in a peaceful settlement to the troubles. They insisted that Captain Jack help them with their plan to ambush and kill the members of the peace commission.

When Canby and his aides arrived, unarmed, at the designated meeting spot, they met eight armed warriors. There wasn't even a short scuffle; the peace commission was gunned down without pause. This was the death knell for Captain Jack and his band.

Before, Captain Jack's plight had gained sympathy both from the Army troops and from the citizens of the area partially because of his group's obvious determination and their obvious high level of survival skills that had allowed them to remain free. General Canby, in particular, had even planned his attacks so that as few Modocs would be harmed as possible. Now, a volunteer group of white settlers joined a newly reinforced Army in defeating Jack by starving his group out of their stronghold and then commencing to loot the fortress and kill an unconfirmed number of women, children, and elderly.

Captain Jack and a small group of Modoc managed to escape the massacre, and they survived on their own for about a month, always pursued by law enforcement. Then, one by one, they surrendered. Jack was the last to turn himself in. Eventually, he would be hanged along with four other members of the group that murdered the peace commission members. The majority of the Modocs were moved to a reservation.

By 1873 when the Modoc Indian War took place, northern California was not really like the Old West portrayed in Cowboy and Indian movies and stories. The Modocs were members of the communities in which they lived, and they lived in houses just like their white neighbors. Most of the men wore blue jeans—the uniform of the California rancher. It was unlikely that the whites who complained of the Indians' looting and livestock depredations had any evidence to back their claims. The Modoc Indian War was a tragedy, both because it didn't have to end as harshly as it did, and because it didn't really have to happen in the first place.

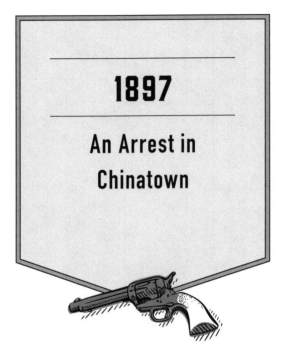

1897

An Arrest in Chinatown

A crowd gathered to watch the scene as a Chinese man in a rough canvas jacket was pulled away by several San Francisco police officers. The man's queue, or long braid usually worn at the nape of the neck, might have been tied up on top of his head in the fashion of the tong "hit men" who had been terrorizing Chinatown since the murder of Fong Ching, who was also called "Little Pete," in January 1897. These tongs, gangs of Chinese immigrants, were often at war with one another, but this time the violence had continued for months, and the police had made little attempt to stop the altercations. Many of the Chinese involved were illegal immigrants engaged in equally illegal business—gambling, prostitution, and the drug trade. To a great extent, the white citizens of San Francisco, including the police, believed it was better for the gangs to war with each other. The more Chinese who were killed by Chinese hands meant fewer for the government to deal with—but arrests were still common on Chinatown's streets.

The attitude of the police, and of most non-Chinese residents of San Francisco, was, in fact, a cause of much of the illegal activity taking place in Chinatown. Before the California gold rush in the late 1840s and early 1850s, only a few immigrants had come to California, but by 1852 there were twenty thousand Chinese immigrants living in San Francisco. At first, these newcomers were welcomed into the community. They worked in San Francisco, providing needed services that had fallen by the wayside with the great exodus of white miners to the gold fields. In the early days of immigration during the gold rush, the Chinese working as domestic help or in laundries were a welcome sight. In fact, the Chinese contingent in San Francisco was even invited to participate in an 1852 Fourth of July parade. They were truly members of the community.

When the Chinese tried their hands at mining in the later days of the gold rush, they met with different attitudes entirely. White miners, many frustrated with their failure at their schemes to gain riches in the hills of California, believed they failed because the Chinese were successful at their own mining ventures and were taking the chance to find gold away from the white miners. Suddenly, the Chinese who had been welcome as laborers such a short time before were accused of stealing the gold and the jobs of hard-working American citizens.

The state of California reacted to what was now perceived as the Chinese menace by restricting immigration through the Exclusion Act. Under the act, only a certain number of merchants and students from Asian countries were allowed to enter the United States every year. These immigrants, and the ones who had come before them, were not allowed citizenship but lived as legal aliens in the United States. Unfortunately, because of the prejudice against the Chinese, it was very difficult for them to find work, and many were forced to turn to illegal activities to support themselves and join the tongs of the most powerful Chinese to protect themselves.

One of the most common illegal activities was smuggling illegal immigrants into the country to work for the tong bosses. The man who was arrested with some difficulty on the street in Chinatown that October was captured outside of 830/832 Washington Street, a notorious first residence for new, illegal immigrants. Many gambling establishments, most of which had been owned by the late Fong Ching, were also in the neighborhood. The man was taken away by police officers and detectives who drove off with him in the police cart as a white and Chinese crowd looked on.

We will never know for certain what the man was arrested for, as arrests of that type were not at all uncommon in late nineteenth century San Francisco. As events go, the arrest of a single man for unknown charges is not a remarkable one. It is particularly unremarkable given the fact that the man was Chinese in a time of turmoil and persecution of the Chinese people in San Francisco and in all of California.

What is remarkable is that this event was captured on film with a very early movie camera. The silent, black-and-white film lasts only about forty-eight seconds, but it speaks volumes about the relationship between the Chinese and whites in San Francisco. Today the sixty-eight feet of 35-mm film are held by the Library of Congress but can be seen on the World Wide Web by visiting http://www.sfmuseum .org/hist1/. The film is an important reminder of a perhaps unnecessarily harsh period in Chinese-American relations.

1906

Flames Amid the Ruins

Alfred Hertz, the conductor of the Metropolitan Opera of New York, ran in a panic to the rooms of his star tenor in San Francisco's Palace Hotel. When he arrived, he saw pieces of a shattered French chandelier scattered on the floor, bureau drawers open and their contents tumbling out into the topsy-turvy room. He sped through the formerly elegant parlor, which looked as though it had been ransacked by burglars, to the bedroom where the great Enrico Caruso was sitting up in his bed, clutching his nightshirt around him like a child afraid of a storm. The tenor had been weeping uncontrollably for some minutes. When Hertz asked him if he had been injured, Caruso became hysterical; he was afraid that the shock from the traumatic experience he had just been through had damaged his voice.

Hertz was confused; Caruso seemed quite able to speak, but perhaps he was still terrified and needed reassurance. He urged the tenor to try his voice, but Caruso replied he could not when the world had collapsed around him. Hertz continued to soothe him. "But the earthquake," he said, "is over."

Reluctantly, Caruso went to the window of his bedroom with the conductor and together they looked down at the mayhem in the streets below. People had fled from the Palace Hotel and the surrounding buildings without even dressing. Many were half-naked in the streets. People were trying desperately to rescue their belongings, their families, and themselves from the calamity that had struck. The noise from the chatter below was more than the tenor could take. He began to weep again at the sight of the destruction below and at the sounds coming through the open window. Hertz would have none of it. He rapped the windowsill sharply and commanded the tenor to sing.

Caruso began with gusto, "*La fanta mi salva/L'immondo ritrova—*" and the people on the street below stopped and stared up at the window. It was a startling performance, and Caruso would not repeat it; instead he used his restored voice to begin a tirade against all of the people who had conspired to bring him to the God-forsaken West and the scene of this tragedy.

Shortly after 5:00 a.m. on April 18, 1906, John B. Farish, another visitor to San Francisco who was staying at the elegant St. Francis Hotel, was shaken awake in his bed. He later recalled:

I was awakened by a loud rumbling noise which might be compared to the mixing sounds of a strong wind rushing through the forest and breaking of waves against a cliff. In less time than it takes to tell, a concussion similar to that caused by the nearby explosion of a huge blast, shook the building to its foundations and then began a series of the liveliest motions imaginable, accompanied by a creaking, grinding, rasping, sound, followed by tremendous crashes as the cornices of adjoining buildings and chimneys tottered to the ground.

The quakes and their aftershocks shook an area from Salinas to Fort Bragg, a distance of two hundred miles. San Francisco was in ruins.

Doors to rooms and whole buildings jammed shut and people were trapped inside badly damaged houses. At the Sonoma Wine Company fifteen million gallons of wine were destroyed. At the Valencia Hotel, the damage from the earthquake was so severe that the building was completely collapsed. Some of the people inside died before help could arrive, drowned in the water from a broken main.

As people recovered from the initial shock, those who could took to the streets and whole families could be seen standing on the sidewalks in their nightclothes. The city was a shambles, and then the fires started all over town.

The alarms at the fire station had broken in the first quake and had ceased to function, but as soon as the ground stopped shaking the horses were harnessed to the engines and the men headed out looking for fires. The men could do no good, however; all but one of the main water arteries into the city had broken in the earthquake, and even if they continued to work, the system of underground pipes that could carry water to hydrants was completely destroyed in the quake. No one ever even knew how many people the earth-quake killed, because the fire swept through before rescuers could get help to people who were trapped.

In desperation people used wine and vinegar to fight the blazes that had started all over town. The sewers were emptied as well. Some people had filled tubs with water as soon as the quake hit, but it wasn't enough.

A fire called the Ham and Eggs fire, because it started when a woman tried to cook breakfast on her quake-damaged stove, was one of the worst, but similar fires started all over town because of the structural damage to chimneys and gas mains caused by the quake. By the time the fires were all under control, when rain came on the 21st of April, more than 490 city blocks had burned. It was the worst conflagration ever, worse even than the fire that burned London in 1604. More than three thousand people died in the earthquake and the subsequent blazes.

One of those who died was Fire Chief Sullivan, who had been severely injured in the quake. He lingered for several days in a coma with a massive head wound caused by the collapse of a brick chimney, but eventually succumbed at the Presidio. He had formed a plan to stop such a conflagration almost immediately upon accepting the job of chief; however, the interim chief, who was not privy to all of the details, was unable to implement it before it was too late. Some reports said the smoke from the fire could be seen one hundred miles out from shore.

As for the great tenor, Enrico Caruso, after the first terror of the morning of April 18 ended, he dressed in a smashing outfit from his impeccable wardrobe, wrapped a towel around his throat to protect it, went out for a large breakfast, then retrieved his sketching pad and a portrait of himself with Theodore Roosevelt, then president of the United States, and went to a hill overlooking the city where he spent hours watching the fires and drawing memorable pictures of the frenzied inhabitants of San Francisco. He knew he would soon be able to leave this terrible city, and go on to the rest of his life in a place untouched by disaster. The calm he exhibited was almost eerie after his scene earlier that morning. Later that day, however, as the crowds swarmed around him, he panicked again.

Somehow, he made his way with the crowds to Golden Gate Park, where a temporary refugee camp was set up for those who needed transportation across the bay and out of the city or just shelter and medical care until the crisis was over. He stumbled through the throngs searching for a familiar face from the touring company, and finally ran across his valet, Martino. Caruso's strong voice became a weak whisper as he pleaded with Martino to get him out of the city immediately. Martino suggested that the photo of Caruso with Roosevelt might gain them some help and he suggested that Caruso hand it over; however, Caruso would not part with it, insisting that it was his passport.

Martino was finally able to arrange for transportation to the ferry that could take them out of San Francisco across the water to Oakland, for the exorbitant cost of $300. But once at the ferry site, it looked as though there was no chance for a berth on the ferry. Finally, Caruso went up to one of the officials on duty and said imperiously, "I am Enrico Caruso, the singer."

The man was not impressed, so Caruso tried another tack and thrust the portrait of himself and the president into his hands. "I am a friend of President Roosevelt. See! He gave me this!"

Another official was attracted by the commotion. When he was told who the strange little man claimed to be, he said, "You Enrico Caruso? Then sing!"

Caruso was flustered. "Sing! I want to leave here!"

The official was nonplussed. "Sure," he said, "but you sing first!"

Caruso obliged, singing a few bars from *Carmen.* A few minutes later, he and his valet boarded the boat for Oakland.

The people he had watched all day, however, left homeless and frantic in the quake and fire, were to be sheltered in a tent city that was hastily set up in Golden Gate Park while the fires were extinguished and their homes were reconstructed. It took seventy-four hours from the time of the quake for most of the fires to be squelched. In San Francisco, almost seven square miles had already been burned and nearly thirty thousand buildings destroyed. For months after, as the recovery progressed, more than forty thousand people slept, cooked, and ate in the tent city in the park waiting for the city to rebuild.

1911

Ishi

Dawn was not quite finished breaking on the morning of August 29, 1911, when the barking of dogs awoke the butchers sleeping near their small slaughterhouse near Oroville. They arose and went to the corral, where they saw a small and obviously frightened figure crouched against the fence.

When they called off the dogs, they saw a terrified man—an Indian—who was horribly emaciated and naked except for a ragged and ancient piece of canvas from a covered wagon that he wore as a poncho. His hair was burned off close to his head, and when they spoke to him, they learned that he could not speak a word of English.

Not knowing what else to do with this stranger, the butchers called the sheriff in Oroville and told him they were holding a wild man. When Sheriff J. B. Webber arrived, he and his men pulled their guns on the man as they handcuffed him. They could tell that the man was exhausted and frightened. So, when they arrived at the county jail, they put him in the cell for the insane, mostly to protect the strange man from curious townsfolk who were already crowded around, hoping for a look.

For his first few days in the jail, the man would not eat or drink—he wouldn't even sleep! Local Indians came to the jail to try and talk to him, but he was unable to understand their languages and they couldn't understand his, either. Finally, two anthropologists, one from Berkeley and one from the University of California in San Francisco, read about him in the paper. Immediately, they came to the conclusion that he must be a Yahi Indian, one of a tribe thought to have been extinct since 1908.

One of the anthropologists, Professor T. T. Waterman, left immediately for Oroville, taking recordings of the language of two related tribes with him to see if the man could understand them. Only one word, *siwini*, which meant yellow pine, was understood by both of them. This man was almost definitely one of the "lost" tribe. Waterman and the Indian—who wished to be called Ishi—became friends over the shared word.

On Labor Day, 1911, Waterman and Ishi went to San Francisco on the train. Ishi was to become a resident at the Anthropology Museum of the University of California Affiliated Colleges, where curious visitors called him the "Wild Man of Oroville" or "Stone Age Man." He was given a pleasant room and a salary of twenty-five dollars a month for performing demonstrations on making bows and arrows, using a fire drill, and other skills Waterman knew that were specific to Ishi's tribe. Waterman and Kroeber, the anthropologists, took many pictures of Ishi and even made films and audio recordings of him. While Ishi was at the museum, the two anthropologists also worked with Ishi to learn his personal story and to find out what had happened to his people.

As EuroAmerican emigrants invaded California in the rush for gold and then as settlement continued to grow in the early years of statehood, the Yana Indians, of which Ishi's small tribe of Yahi were a part, were increasingly pushed off of their ancestral land and into smaller and smaller territories away from their traditional homes. The Yahi, in particular, were forced into areas where they could not live off the land as they had always done, and so they had resorted to thievery and livestock depredation in order to survive. The white settlers thought they were justified in killing these desperate people in an attempt to protect their property. On the morning of August 16, 1865, the Yahi were attacked in response to these thefts and murders, and almost the entire group was wiped out. The Yahi had never been more than three-hundred or four-hundred people strong, and, by 1872, it was thought that they all had been exterminated. In fact, about twelve were left, and Ishi was among them.

Ishi had been a small boy in the 1860s and 1870s when times had been the worst for the Yahi. His only memories of living with his tribe were of terror—both from fear of the whites and fear of starvation. When he was about ten years old, in the early 1870s, the twelve remaining Yahi, including Ishi and his mother, entered into complete hiding. The whites simply never saw them again until about 1908.

By then, slowly, the twelve men, women, and children had become only four. The others had died from old age, starvation, and fear. Only Ishi, his mother, a sister or cousin, and an old man were left. They were already desperate when a surveying party came upon them in November 1908, surprising them into abandoning their possessions and running for cover. All of their possessions were taken by the surveyors, who came back to look for the Yahi but never found them. When they scattered, Ishi and his mother were separated from the old man and young woman. Ishi later said he believed them to be dead. Not too long before he was found in the corral, Ishi's mother died, and he was left completely alone. His hair was burned off in mourning for his mother.

Ishi was understandably afraid of the men at the slaughterhouse that day. After all, whites had murdered nearly all of his people. Surely, he thought he would be killed—shot, hanged, or poisoned—if he let his guard down. But by the time he collapsed in the corral that morning, he might have been beyond caring whether he lived or died. He was completely alone in the world, and he wouldn't have even recognized the world he now lived in when he came out of hiding. That day at the slaughterhouse was Ishi's first real exposure to the twentieth century. Called the "last wild man in North America," he boarded the train and headed for his new life at the museum.

Ishi lived and worked at the museum in San Francisco for four years and seven months, until his death from tuberculosis on March 25, 1916. His tenure there was a happy one. He learned English, was able to tell the story of his people, and had a fascination with modern technology. He was much beloved by museum visitors and staff, and there was an outpouring of affection for him after his death.

During his life at the museum, Ishi never said his Yahi name. It was simply not the custom for California Indians to give up that particular piece of information. He allowed them to call him Ishi, which simply means "man."

1913

The Wolf House Burns

Jack London, adventurer, sailor, and world-famous author, was giddy with delight. Full of pride, he watched as the workers finished polishing the redwood and swept up wood shavings. He and his wife, Charmian, could begin moving all of their collected treasures into the beautiful house the next day. After three years, the Wolf House was finally ready!

The wonderful dream house—the house that Jack planned as a permanent monument to himself—had consumed his imagination and attention during those three years. It had a beautiful library to house his thousands of books, a study for his work, a music room, a gargantuan dining room to seat his frequent guests and a dozen bedrooms to host them overnight, and a cavernous basement recreation room for their rowdier activities. The building materials would be the giant redwoods from his ranch in the Valley of the Moon and the red rocks that formed the hillsides. Jack intended for the beautiful house to last forever so that his grandchildren and their grandchildren could appreciate it and understand it as a symbol of him.

Planning and building a beautiful dream like the Wolf House must have been wonderful for Jack London, for although he was now a famous author, he had endured many hardships and disappointments in his life. He had been born in San Francisco in 1876, and had to start working to support his family when he was only ten years old. He sold newspapers and worked in a cannery, then he bought a boat and became an oyster pirate, and then he signed on as a sailor on either a whaling boat that sailed off the coast of Siberia or a sealer that headed for Japan. His money and luck always seemed to run out, meaning the end of every adventure! Finally he returned to San Francisco, where he worked for ten cents an hour as a coal heaver.

The world might never have heard of Jack London, but after years of tramping about and working at menial jobs, he finally decided to go back to school. Jack had always been an avid reader, and he was able to complete high school and pass college entrance examinations in a year and a half. He then enrolled at the University of California at Berkeley and spent a few months there before he heard the call of the Klondike Gold Rush.

Attempting the adventure of the Klondike was a turning point in Jack's life. When he came back, he was unable to find a steady job in Oakland, but his head was teeming with stories. For months he wrote for nineteen hours a day, sending his tales of adventure in the cold north to the popular magazines of the day. Finally, after months and months of collecting rejection slips, he made his first sale. The *Overland Monthly* bought a story called "To the Man on the Trail" for five whole dollars. Jack London was finally launched as an author. Within ten years, he became one of the highest-paid, most famous writers in America.

Even though Jack was a famous author, he had also suffered other disappointments. He was married in 1900 and had two daughters, but he was divorced from their mother in 1905 and lost almost all contact with them. He remarried later in 1905, and he and his wife, Charmian, settled on a ranch that Jack purchased near Glen Ellyn, and which he named the Valley of the Moon.

Jack finally thought he could be happy, but he always spent more than he earned as a writer and his hopes for a family that he could pass his name on to were disappointed when his wife had a baby girl who died within three days in 1910.

But, Jack thought, all of that was behind them now, and they could start life anew. The dream house that he had lovingly planned was finally finished and ready for their belongings! They spent the night in the old ranch house on the Valley of the Moon ranch, knowing that it would be their last. But at two o'clock in the morning, Jack and Charmian were awakened by shrill screams. They could hear the sickening sounds of the flames and the voices yelling, "Fire! Fire!"

Jack ran to the top of a hill and saw the house that he called "the most beautiful home in America" devoured by flames. There was no water to stop the blaze. All Jack could do was sit and watch as his dreams vanished. He put his face in his hands and wept.

Jack believed—he knew—that someone had deliberately set fire to his new, beautiful home. There was no other explanation. He had planned for the house to be fireproof, part of his dream for it to last forever. Jack suspected many people of lighting the fire deliberately just to hurt him, but the builder claimed that it must have been a case of spontaneous combustion. Jack simply could not revive himself from the disappointment of losing his dream—not even long enough to ferret out the cause of the blaze or to discover the guilty party if there was one. He never attempted to rebuild.

From the time that the Wolf House burned, Jack London seemed to sink further and further into depression. He was unable to work at his previous pace, and eyed with suspicion guests who came to his house, thinking that one of them might be the person who had set the fire.

Although from time to time Jack was able to recover some of his old vigor, he never fully recovered from his greatest disappointment. He died in 1916 after taking an overdose of some medicine. It is not known whether his death was intentional.

Jack's dreams of being remembered after his death were realized, whether his dream house outlived him or not. When he died, the European press gave his demise more space than they did the death of Emperor Francis Joseph of Austria—who had died just the day before. His wife, Charmian, built another house at the Valley of the Moon, The House of Happy Walls, which is a monument to Jack and his work.

1922

Silence at the Mystery House

A t first, the changes and additions Sarah Winchester had wanted seemed reasonable enough. If there were not enough guest rooms in her San Jose mansion, another wing could be added to the already extensive house. The grounds were big enough to hold another mansion. If there were a need for another dining room to accommodate a favorite antique table, it could be added as well. The carpenters were happy to keep hammering and sawing and also happy to keep collecting paychecks. It was an interesting job in beautiful, sunny, warm San Jose, and Mrs. Winchester had the money to do everything she wanted, whether it seemed normal or not.

Sarah Winchester, heir to the Winchester Rifle fortune, bought what would become the Winchester Mystery House in 1884. Created out of an old farmhouse, her new home was to be a grand estate, situated on a large plot of land in the rolling hills of San Jose, California. The house would be the biggest, most elaborate, highly decorated home in the city—more impressive than the great mansions of San Francisco. People were sure Sarah intended to fill it with the finest antiques and artwork from around the world and to share its glittering ballroom, massive dining rooms, and bedrooms and baths with hundreds of guests.

Sarah moved in to be surrounded by the construction as soon as she was able. Although she had no family, no one to share the enormous house with her, she seemed perfectly content. The carpenters continued their banging and sawing, and every day she made changes to her plans according to her whim. Sarah was a busy woman; with a hundred workers at her beck and call, she had a full-time job in completing her house but she claimed she had help—in the spirit friends who were guiding her every decision.

In 1862, Sarah Pardee had married William Wirt Winchester, son of the famous gun manufacturer, in New Haven, Connecticut. Within a month of her infant daughter's birth, in 1863, the baby died and Sarah was inconsolable. Fifteen years was not enough to soothe her sorrow; when her still-young husband died in 1878, she knew that her life was soon to be over, as well. She believed that a curse must be on her and her family.

A psychic in Boston convinced Sarah that unless she went west to the land where the Winchester Rifle had done its most damage and built a house for the spirits of those killed by the rifles, she would never be safe from death, herself. The psychic explained that the spirits of people killed by the Winchester Rifle were haunting her and had killed her family. The poor souls of the people who had died at the end of the source of her fortune needed a resting place on earth, and as long as she continued building her house, as long as she added more room for their souls to occupy, she would be protected from harm. If she didn't try to give the good spirits a home, and trick the evil spirits so that they couldn't find her, something terrible would happen. Sarah became convinced that she could actually prevent her own death if the building on her house never stopped.

Sarah's belief in the occult was not uncommon for her time; many people in the nineteenth century believed strongly in the existence of ghosts and spirits that could visit or haunt the living. Mary Todd Lincoln had a strong belief in the supernatural, and she had even held seances in the White House during the Civil War! Many other fashionable, wealthy people also believed the fortunetellers and mystics who claimed they could contact dead relatives or predict the end of the world. Rich men and women paid the psychics well to tell them what they wanted to hear, or to frighten them.

Sarah Winchester may have believed more strongly than most, however. At night, in her lonely house, with all of the workers gone for the day, she spoke to her spirit friends in a room carefully designed for that purpose. There was only one door into the room, but there were three ways out if she needed to escape evil spirits; of course one of the doors out dropped straight down to a kitchen sink on the floor below and the other was a one-way trap door.

Sarah chose beautiful furnishings for all of her magnificent rooms, and the modern conveniences she had planned, such as the electric lights and hot and cold taps in the guest bathrooms, worked splendidly. Many of the windows were made from her own designs—daisies and spider webs were her favorite motifs. She also loved the number thirteen. If a candelabra held only twelve candles, she would alter it to accommodate another. Even the drains in sinks were not ignored—most had thirteen holes.

The builders complied with all of Sarah's requests, which became stranger and stranger. She claimed that spirit friends were guiding her decisions. She added rooms to the house wherever she could, even if it meant that windows looked into other rooms instead of out onto the grounds. She added staircases that did not take you to another floor, doors that looked like they concealed closets or other rooms but actually opened into walls; there were even rooms that had no way in, and no way out.

As long as the house remained unfinished, Sarah felt safe from her ghosts. If she could just keep building her house, she reasoned, she would never die. She added cornices and sun rooms and staircases and windows as long as the workers kept coming every day, to add another room, another detail to the Winchester Mansion.

The builders kept coming, but the house was never finished. In spite of her best intentions and efforts, Sarah Winchester died in 1922—apparently of ripe old age, not from a run-in with evil spirits. The architects, builders, decorators, and pipe fitters were busy at her house for thirty-eight years. When she died, the building stopped.

The house, now known as the Winchester Mystery House, takes up six acres and has more than one hundred sixty rooms. There are almost as many new ghost stories associated with the house as there are windows and doors within. Some visitors and tour guides at the Winchester Mystery House say they have seen old Mrs. Winchester herself walking the hallways and wringing her hands. They say she is worried about the souls of the people she left homeless when the building finally stopped. Others say she just watches the visitors who stream in every day, laughing at her monumental joke. The thought of the tiny, fretful woman who had built this crazy house with its many extra staircases, windows, and doors is amusing, and the secrets of her mystery house genuinely perplex many guests who tour it every day.

The visitors who stand on the stairs in the mansion today can contemplate the sad, lonely life that Sarah Winchester must have had in this enormous house with its haunting spirits. Maybe she just invented the ghost stories to keep her real visitors—the men and women who worked for her for thirty-eight years—coming to see her. As they stand on the stairs and chuckle, today's visitors can also think about the fun Sarah must have had hanging on for one more year, one more grand ballroom or guest bath, another parlor, or just another day with the crowds of workers around her, working just for her. And now, the crowds keep coming.

1937

The Opening of the Golden Gate Bridge

Typical San Francisco fog obscured the bright International Orange towers, and wind whipped men's neckties around their faces and threatened ladies' hats as thousands of people thronged to the finally completed Golden Gate Bridge and paid 25 cents to be among the first people to set foot on its walkways and make the 4,200-foot trek from San Francisco to Marin County. For four years, residents had watched and listened as the massive structure seemed to emerge from the depths of San Francisco Bay. And May 27, 1937, was a day of celebration and achievement for the crews, the engineers, the supporters of the bridge—and for the people of the city who had been enduring the hardest years of the Great Depression.

As early as 1872, officials and builders and engineers and architects had begun talking about the possibility of bridging the nearly mile-wide Golden Gate Strait and connecting the city with the Marin Headlands to the north. The relatively short span of water seemed to beg for a structure or system to make it easy to cross, and designs were suggested beginning around 1916, but it wasn't until the 1920s and the expansion of personal and commercial traffic due to the rise of the automobile that public opinion was swayed to accept the advantages and support the financing of such a bridge. The first design proposal was submitted by a Cincinnati-based engineer by the name of Joseph Strauss, who suggested a combination cantilever and suspension bridge with a relatively modest price tag of $27 million.

Suddenly, the idea seemed possible—and over the next decade, the design evolved and changed as Strauss worked with an architect named Irving Morrow and an engineer named Leon Moisseiff. Moisseiff further developed the idea of the suspension bridge, and the design was eventually selected. Morrow and his wife, Gertrude, designed the Art Deco superstructure, and in 1929, Strauss was chosen to be the chief engineer on the project. Morrow would also eventually help choose the iconic International Orange color to complement the surrounding area and the beautiful sunsets.

Formed in 1928, the Golden Gate Bridge and Highway District united San Francisco, Sonoma, Del Norte, Marin, and parts of Mendocino and Napa counties in the effort to fund the bridge. The idea was straightforward—they would take a collective bond or loan to fund the project and then repay it through bridge tolls. Then, in October 1929, the stock market crashed, and the United States was plunged into the Great Depression.

Still, the visionaries behind the bridge forged ahead and the community rallied behind the project. A year after the stock market crash, in November 1930, the residents of the area contained in the Golden Gate Bridge and Highway district agreed to use their farms, businesses, and even homes as collateral to support a $35 million bond. The intention was to repay the bond through the tolls that would be charged to travelers crossing the bridge.

On January 5, 1933, when construction finally began, the toll of the Great Depression and the effects of the migration of residents of the so-called "Dust Bowl" states to California and other areas were being felt nationwide. Breaking ground on a massive project was both a financial boost to the area because of the jobs it provided and a psychological boost to a community that could finally see progress happening in the San Francisco Bay after years of discussion.

Even though the distance that the bridge had to span was relatively short—it would also require a structure that would end up being the longest bridge in the world at the time it was completed. The concepts behind a suspension bridge weren't new—but applying them to such a length and in the conditions that the builder faced would provide new challenges.

First, California is earthquake prone, as the residents of San Francisco remembered vividly from the 1906 earthquake that had devastated the city and changed it forever. A suspension bridge made for a sensible choice in a seismically active region as it allowed the structure to sway a certain amount without structural damage. Workers had to blast out rock 65 feet below the surface of the strait to place foundations that would withstand an earthquake. The flexibility of the bridge was also important due to the high winds frequently experienced in the San Francisco region, which would also complicate the construction itself. Fog, frequent storms, and the sheer size of the bridge made construction a feat of human and scientific progress. Eleven men would die during the construction.

When it was finished, at 4,200 feet, it was the longest bridge in the world, and it would retain that title until the Verazzano-Narrows Bridge opened in New York City in 1964. Once the Golden Gate Bridge opened, despite fog and wind, the people came in the thousands to pay their toll to walk across its span and look out over the city and the bay. The next day, President Franklin D. Roosevelt opened the bridge for the first time to automobile traffic.

In May 1987, nearly 300,000 people crossed the bridge on foot to commemorate the fiftieth anniversary of its opening—and despite earthquakes and time and weather and other threats, the bridge remains a critical part of Bay-area infrastructure and is also one of the most recognizable symbols of Northern California and the United States around the world, as well as one of the most photographed.

1941

Statehood for Jefferson

The sounds of the Yreka girls' drum and bugle corps could be heard all over town in the cool December air. Cannons were fired, punctuating the shouted sentences of an enthusiastic crowd with their booms. Men, women, and children, dressed in "Western" clothes, carrying signs and handbills proclaiming Independence filled the streets in front of the Siskiyou County Courthouse. And a young boy wearing a coonskin cap led two bear cubs up to the courthouse lawn, where one of them had a photo op with the new territorial governor, John C. Childs, who had been elected two days previously. The crowd had gathered for the inauguration of Childs and the introduction of a new territorial government on December 4, 1941, ready to lead the call for secession from California and statehood for the region that had come to be known as the State of Jefferson.

The area that the state of California covers is enormous—bigger than all of New England plus several other states combined. When it became a state in 1850, after the fastest settlement-to-statehood path since the Articles of Confederation, due largely to the 1849 gold rush, it had grown from a region with scattered, small population centers around Spanish missions to a bustling, though still largely rural region with a relatively small population but already enormous political and economic power relative to its youth and size, underlined by its importance to the Compromise of 1850, which allowed its entry into the Union as a free state. The boom and bust of the Gold Rush had residents flock to the northern part of the state, particularly the region around Yreka, only to leave for the more developed urban centers to the south when the gold ran out. Far northern California, remote already, was difficult to reach due to inferior roads and sheer distance. While the rest of the state developed quickly, growing industries and an economy, the far north was left to fend for itself, unable to take full advantage of its timber and agricultural land, left behind by a legislature that increasingly represented interests in the populous area to the south.

Not long after the Civil War, the first discussions were had about whether California's sheer size and population made it a candidate for being split into two or more separate states. Proposals, ideas, and campaigns surfaced repeatedly for decades, and by 1941, residents of California's Siskiyou, Del Norte, Lassen, and Trinity counties had been long disappointed by their representation in the state government in Sacramento and in the way that they felt forgotten by the more populous regions to the south. Similarly, some southern Oregon counties, including Curry, Josephine, Jackson, and Klamath, felt disenfranchised from the rest of Oregon. Rural areas were still recovering from the effects of the Great Depression, and the restlessness and dissatisfaction grew from a rumble to a movement, until in October 1941, the mayor of Port Orford, Oregon, Gilbert Gable, proposed to combine those counties in California and Oregon into a new state—the State of Jefferson.

The land area in the newly proposed State of Jefferson was roughly the size of West Virginia—a precedent for the kind of move that those voters wanted to make. And Yreka, the county seat of Siskiyou County, California, became the center of the secession movement. Men erected blockades just south of town marked with the words "State of Jefferson Border Patrol," stopping cars that traveled north into town and handing out copies of their "Proclamation of Independence," before allowing them to continue on. And plans were made to hold an election of a governor to lead the movement.

When Gilbert Gable, the Oregon mayor who had proposed the combining of counties, died on December 2, 1941, it was just after he had learned that the Trinity (California) County Board of Supervisors had voted to join other secessionists who were already hard at work. Siskiyou County (California) quickly followed suit, and elections were set for December 4, 1941, in Yreka. Three candidates were put forth for the office of provisional governor of the new state, and John C. Childs, a seventy-eight-year-old judge from Crescent City in Del Norte County, was elected. The inauguration of the new governor would be a spectacle captured by four separate Hollywood film crews who arrived on the scene to make newsreels of the event.

School was canceled for the day as the residents of Yreka and the surrounding areas gathered for a torchlight parade to celebrate the new governor and the start of a real move to separate from the rest of the state. Governor Childs spoke eloquently to the assembly, who stood with their signs raised bearing slogans like "California Forgot Us" and "The Promised Land—Our Roads Are Paved with Promises." Roads were, in fact, a key issue for the residents of the region. In order to take advantage of the timber and mineral wealth of the region, they needed a way to transport resources out of the region. Childs and the other new state officials met immediately on December 6 to begin to plan for the movement's next steps. Spirits were high and the mood was celebratory—perhaps Jefferson would get some traction. The men planned to announce their secession on December 8, with the wide release of the newsreels of the event in Yreka and press coverage across the country.

Unfortunately, the newsreel produced that day in December was destined never to be widely released. The Japanese bombing of Pearl Harbor on December 7 put a halt to the celebrations in Yreka and to further secession talk for the duration of World War II. Still, the idea of the State of Jefferson has never totally faded away. In the 1990s, a suggestion was made to split California into two separate states. And there are other proposals that call for five to seven different states to be carved out of the vast region. The idea isn't a new one or even unique to California. Counties and groups of counties in different states have often suggested similar schemes over the years, from oil- and gas-rich counties that have watched revenues flow into state coffers while their own infrastructure needs are neglected because of lack of representation. And in Northern California, there are still those who argue that the state has benefited from the agricultural and timber bounty of the northern part of the state while their infrastructure needs have been ignored. Even today, counties still talk about the idea of the State of Jefferson. In 2013, Modoc and Siskiyou counties both voted to secede from the larger state of California. In June 2014, Del Norte, Tehama, and Siskiyou counties all had ballot measures related to secession before voters, two of which failed, and in 2015, town hall meetings were being held across the region to stir up the idea of secession. And today, when you drive into Northern California or Southern Oregon, you may still see the signs decreeing that you're in the State of Jefferson.

1943

The Loyalty Question

There were forty-two questions on the papers that had just been passed around to the surprised inhabitants of the camp at Tule Lake, California. The questions were long, and for those who were not native speakers of English, very confusing. Once they were made to understand the substance of Question 28, however, most of the *Issei*, or first-generation Japanese immigrants, had no choice but to answer, "No."

On December 7, 1941, Japanese pilots flying overhead attacked the United States Naval Base at Pearl Harbor, Hawaii, without warning. Within what seemed like minutes of the attack, the United States was officially at war with Japan, and Japanese immigrants all over the United States began to hear rumors that they were to be moved from their homes—which were mostly on the West Coast—and into secure areas away from the temptation to aid their home country through spying or sabotage.

Before even two months had passed, the Japanese found the rumors to be true. President Franklin Roosevelt had signed Executive Order number 9066, which called for the evacuation of all Japanese from the West Coast and their relocation into temporary camps in the interior of the United States. By June, more than 120,000 Japanese-Americans were living in crude barracks behind barbed wire in some of the most desolate locations the West had to offer. More than seventy-one thousand of the Japanese were *Nisei*, the American-born children of Japanese immigrants—citizens of the United States.

The camp at Tule Lake, one of the largest of the relocation camps with nearly 20,000 residents, wasn't on a lake at all. The small barracks where whole families would live together in a single twenty-by-twenty-five-foot room were built on ancient rocky lava beds. Unlike some of the other relocation camps, like the one at Manzanar in southern California, it did not get extremely hot in the summer at Tule Lake, but the winters were extremely long and extremely cold. Temperatures were often well below zero, and the hastily constructed barracks with their thin, temporary walls provided little insulation against the cold.

At first both Issei, Japanese immigrants who had been born in Japan, and Nisei, the children of these immigrants who had been born in America and were American citizens, lived together at the Tule Lake camp. It seemed unbelievable to both groups that they had been subjected to such harsh treatment. Most of the Issei had been in the United States for many years, and many had beautiful homes and successful businesses that they were forced to leave when the relocation order came. Many of the Nisei were shocked and horrified that they, as American citizens, could be removed from their homes and their schools and forced to live in these tiny rooms with only army cots and straw mattresses for furniture. They had been born in the United States and had lived here their whole lives—they were Japanese only by ancestry. The Issei and Nisei had barely even been given time to store their household goods or sell them before being required to report to the relocation camps. They were told to bring only the necessities of life that they could carry to the camps. Most lost nearly everything they had during their internment.

There was a third group of Japanese-Americans known as the *Kibei*, who were American citizens because they had been born in the United States, but who remained loyal to Japan. Many of the Kibei had been sent to Japan by their parents to be educated and had only recently come back to the United States. While all three groups protested their captivity, this group was thought by the government to make the most trouble, and a plan was launched to relocate all Kibei and all Issei and Nisei who remained loyal to Japan to the Tule Lake camp.

That was where the loyalty question, Question Number 28, came in. It asked:

> Will you swear unqualified allegiance to the United States of America and forswear any form of allegiance or obedience to the Japanese emperor, or any other foreign government, power, or organization?

For most of the Kibei, the answer was obvious—they said, "No" and asked to be repatriated to Japan after the war.

For the Issei and the Nisei, however, there were greater issues at stake.

According to United States law, the Issei were not allowed to become American citizens. If they answered "Yes" to Question 28, they would become people without a country; they would no longer be citizens of Japan, but they would still never be able to become citizens of the United States. In addition, the Issei at Tule Lake knew that a "No" answer would keep them at the camp, a little nearer their California homes, rather than be relocated to the Midwest or East Coast. The Nisei, most of whom wished to remain loyal to the United States, were torn because of their devotion to their parents. If they answered "Yes," but their parents answered "No," they would be separated and, for all they knew, would never see them again.

All over the United States, in relocation camps in Montana, Wyoming, California, Utah, and Arkansas, the Japanese prisoners were struggling with the question. Those at Tule Lake who made their decision to remain loyal to the United States were shipped out of the Tule Lake camp and eventually were allowed to leave the camps and settle in cities in the interior of the country. Some of the Nisei men who answered "Yes" even joined the Army to fight in World War II.

Those who answered "No," from around the United States, which included people from all three groups, were removed to the Tule Lake camp, which became a segregation camp—holding only those Japanese who remained loyal to Japan—until its closure on March 20, 1946, after the end of the war.

A number of Issei, Nisei, and Kibei did renounce their American citizenship after the war; many of that number came from the Tule Lake camp, where loyalty had been the highest after the change to segregation. Many of the Issei who answered Question 28 with a resounding "No!" remained in the United States and tried to get a semblance of their old lives back.

What is remarkable, perhaps, is the number of Issei and Nisei who did remain loyal to the United States throughout their internment, even though their adopted country and country by birth, respectively, had betrayed them. After the war, two separate investigations by the Federal Bureau of Investigation and the Federal Communications Commission revealed that there had not been a single case of espionage or sabotage committed by a Japanese American.

1960

The Olympics Go to Squaw Valley

The men of the First Marine Division of the United States Army soberly rode the chair lift to the top of the ski run dressed in full winter gear. When they reached the top they got off the lift, turned around, and skied down the mountain in perfect formation. From overhead, they looked like a flock of geese headed south for the winter, arranged in a perfect "V."

The marines had been brought into Squaw Valley for extremely hazardous duty. It was their job to make sure that the six ski runs were in tiptop shape for the Winter Olympic Games, and every day they rode to the top of the ski lift to pack down the day's snowfall and smooth out the runs.

In 1954, Squaw Valley was a small lodge, almost unknown to all but a few of the most dedicated downhill buffs, when its owner, Alexander Cochrane Cushing, a former lawyer from

New York City, put in a bid for Squaw Valley to host the 1960 Olympic games. When he started his campaign, the forty-five-year-old ski bum and his partner, Wayne Poulson, had a small lodge with one ski tow, accommodations for about 150 people, not enough roads into and out of the lodge, a permanent population of eight, and a lot of potential. Cushing had seen a notice that the U.S. Olympic Committee was looking for candidates to compete against other nations for the site of the 1960 Winter Games, and he thought it was an opportune time for a little extra advertising from the news his bid would generate. He sat down and wrote an eight-page "hymn to the glories of Squaw Valley" for the committee—just as a publicity stunt.

To Cushing's surprise, a few days later he was contacted and asked to make a presentation before the U.S. Olympic Committee. He went to the governor of California to ask for the state's support if the Olympics should come there, and once he received the go-ahead, he nearly sprinted to New York to make the case for the area as a site.

Cushing must have used all of his skills of persuasion before the committee, because Squaw Valley, a little place no one had heard of before this stunt, beat out Nevada's Snow Bowl in Reno; Anchorage, Alaska; Aspen, Colorado; and Lake Placid, New York, as the United States' nominee. Cushing and his wife became the two-person committee that would take the bid for the proposed site to the International Olympic Committee.

The Cushings had almost no support from any participating country except the United States when they arrived in Paris. Everyone thought that Innsbruck, Austria, would definitely be the site of the 1960 Olympics. After all, Squaw

Valley was an obscure California ski resort, and Innsbruck was world-famous for its skiing. In addition, Innsbruck had lost its bid for the 1956 Winter Olympics by a tiny margin.

Still, Cushing and his wife went to Paris to meet with the International Olympic Committee and to tell of the wonders of Squaw Valley. They took along a scale model of the valley that showed the way the site would look in time for the 1960 games, and then found that it was too big to fit in the display room where the other displays were being shown. The U.S. embassy had to quickly rent another room for the display, and the disgruntled committee members were forced to visit it separately from the other exhibitors. That accident may have made all the difference. Alone in its own room, the display stood out from the competitors. Squaw Valley was chosen as the site for the 1960 Olympics on the second ballot.

It would cost approximately sixteen million dollars to remake the Squaw Valley resort area into a site befitting the Olympic Games. But before the work was barely started, trouble began between Cushing and his partner, Wayne Poulson. Poulson opposed the plans for the Olympic games, and a bitter argument developed between Poulson and Cushing. Poulson, at first, refused to allow the games to go on, but he was eventually convinced to sell some key land holdings to the Olympic committee and to lease others. Then Cushing was asked to do the same and to remove himself from the planning. He did, and then gracefully backed away. The plans for the Winter Olympics would finally take shape.

The Marines were not the only group that pitched in to help convert Squaw Valley into the Olympic wonderland. The Navy came in and built a parking lot of packed snow, water, and sawdust near the areas where the ski runs were located. When finished it would hold twelve thousand cars. As the landscape was remade, the organizing committee had a brainstorm about the pageantry that would accompany the games, especially the opening and closing ceremonies. Prentis Hale, the president of the organizing committee, went to Walt Disney himself for help. When Disney was approached in the middle of all the fighting over the plans and the site, he said, "In fact, I've got a great idea for the closing ceremony now. We mount a huge loudspeaker on top of Squaw Peak (8,995 feet) and we blast out an unearthly noise. The noise starts an avalanche, the avalanche wipes out the valley, and that way everybody stops fighting." But he planned a spectacle for the opening ceremonies that included five thousand performers, fifty-two California and Nevada high school bands, fireworks, and the release of two thousand pigeons that would represent doves of peace. Disney workers built an eighty-foot "Tower of Nations" where the Olympic torch would be kept, and thirty snow statues, each sixteen feet high, decorated the valley.

By the time the opening ceremonies commenced, everything was in place—in spite of the fact that it hadn't snowed as much as everyone would have liked—and the 1960 Winter Olympics were underway. On February 18, 1960, thirty-five thousand spectators and eight hundred athletes from thirty-four nations converged upon Alex Cushing's resort to see the amazing feats on the ski slopes and on the ice rink and to view beautiful Squaw Valley.

1962

Bodega Bay Goes to *The Birds*

It was a quiet afternoon in the tiny village of Bodega Bay, and some children had gathered on the lawn of a house for a birthday party. The cake had just been brought out to the decorated picnic table when the children began a game of "blind-man's bluff." The birthday girl was blindfolded, and she began her silent search for the other children.

Suddenly, the sky was filled with a mass of screeching seagulls. The large white birds, common to the area, screamed like angry cats as they swept down toward the children and began pecking at them with their sharp beaks. The children and the adults present at the party ran for cover in the house, after having to beat the determined birds off of them.

Of course, this attack in Bodega Bay didn't really happen; nor did the myriad other bird attacks portrayed in the sleepy village take place. Crows, chickens, gulls, and all of the other birds in the area were given the starring role—as the villains—in the famous Alfred Hitchcock film where the birds of the air suddenly turn on the people below.

Bodega Bay must have seemed the perfect place to film the suspense film, which has since become a classic of American cinema. The town was not much more than a general store, restaurant, and clapboard schoolhouse with a white cupola on top when Hitchcock chose it for the setting for the movie. The few buildings, blue sky, green hills, and sandy dunes must have seemed to fit the need for an isolated setting completely. As the schoolteacher, Annie Hayworth, said in the film, "There's a lot of spare time in Bodega Bay."

The residents of the village must have been surprised to see the transformation in their tiny town once it hit the big screen, however. After the initial filming was complete in Bodega Bay, the actors and crew returned to a film studio in Hollywood to complete the work on the film. Once there, the birds were contained within what was a described as a large polyethylene bag, which kept them from flying into the equipment and wreaking havoc with the lights and cameras.

Crew men persuaded the birds to perform in the air with bits of food, while the actors below were given a fairly gruesome task. They were asked to hold bits of hamburgers in their hands while shielding their eyes, in order to get the birds to peck at their faces and make it look like the birds were attacking them. But that wasn't the strangest thing they were asked to do. In one scene where a flock of crows chases a crowd of schoolchildren, the birds were actually tied to the child-actors' backs. Luckily a representative of the Humane

Society was on hand to make sure the birds were not injured or too tired by their work.

Through movie magic, Alfred Hitchcock's crew was able to make it look like birds took over the village of Bodega Bay. The birds lined the telephone and electric wires outside of houses, and in one particularly frightening scene, they covered a jungle gym in the playground at the school. They swooped down out of the air and attacked people in boats, and even killed a few of the movie characters.

The strangest thing about the movie was that the actions of the birds were never explained. Several causes for their strange behavior were hinted at but none explored. There was a good reason for it. In spite of the fact that Hitchcock claimed the movie was just based on a short story by Daphne du Maurier, it was actually also inspired by a similar event that had taken place in Santa Cruz only the year before. There, birds had swooped down out of the sky, hitting people in the head, crashing into poles, and hitting the doors of people's houses. There was no explanation for the birds' strange behavior.

That is, there was no explanation until much later. It seems that the gulls in Santa Cruz had ingested too much of a chemical in monosodium glutamate, and it had caused a malfunction in their brains that led to the strange behavior. For the effectiveness of the movie, however, viewers only needed to know that the birds had suddenly turned on people.

1965

Saving a Legend
Starts a Trend

Stanford's fall semester was yet to start in August 1965 when Fritz Maytag, a graduate student in literature, went into a bar and ordered his favorite beer, Anchor Steam. Fritz had been drinking Anchor Steam since he had come to the West Coast from Iowa, and he looked up in surprise when the bartender said, "Enjoy. It could be your last."

It seemed that the old brewery, which had been in business in one incarnation or another since the 1860s, was finally bankrupt and they would be closing their doors in about a week. That is, they would have closed their doors had Fritz Maytag not received the disturbing news of their imminent demise. It was a lucky coincidence for the Anchor Brewery and for beer lovers everywhere. Fritz Maytag, heir to the Maytag Appliance Fortune, sold a few of his shares in the family business and kept the brewery afloat.

The Anchor Brewery had been in San Francisco since the 1860s, and had gone by the name Anchor—producing the highly acclaimed Anchor Steam—since the 1890s. It was started in a time when small breweries existed by the thousands in the United States. In 1873, there were 4,131 local breweries and every area had its own special brand of beer.

However, in 1920 the United States added an amendment to the Constitution that all but quashed small breweries in the United States. For thirteen years, the Sixteenth Amendment, Prohibition, was the law of the land. Before Prohibition laws were passed, almost every town of any size, and some much smaller, could boast their own brand of locally brewed beer. However, most small breweries were unable to bear the burden of the thirteen dry years and went out of business. Only the breweries that were able to convert their assets in the form of equipment and labor into a business that produced something other than beer stayed alive.

When Prohibition was over in 1933, only a few breweries were left, and they were the big names that ruled the industry for most of the twentieth century. Miller, Anheuser-Busch, and others emerged from their various other incarnations and took over the beer industry. Through mass production of the beer, the creation of uniformly flavored products, and the ability to transport beer quickly and easily via trucks and trains, the bigger breweries put any Prohibition-surviving smaller brewery out of business. Most buildings and equipment simply stood idle for years.

Most of the smaller breweries simply couldn't afford to follow where the big conglomerates were going, but a few, like Anchor Brewing, had stayed alive, and had a following among the locals able to sample their beers.

However, there was still some mystique about carefully handcrafted beers, available only regionally, in the United States. With that in mind, Fritz Maytag purchased the old Anchor Brewery in San Francisco and started a trend that has changed beer drinking in the United States almost as much as Prohibition did.

When Fritz Maytag first invested in Anchor in 1965, his only interest was in keeping the business open, not necessarily running it himself, but in 1969, he bought the brewery outright and became its brewmaster and president. What he actually bought was slightly less than impressive, a homemade copper kettle, a crude combination mash tun and lauter tun, three steel tanks that weren't refrigerated and appeared to have been painted on the inside with some kind of wood stain, and the recipe for Anchor Steam.

It wasn't impossible to brew with the outdated equipment, but it certainly wasn't easy. Maytag would go around to the five big breweries in the San Francisco area and buy yeast from them, alternating with every batch. At that point, he said, he was more interested in creating something drinkable than something consistent.

In 1965, the brewery had produced around six hundred barrels of Anchor Steam, the only recipe it used. But in the early 1970s, Maytag decided to branch out, and his decision turned the brewery around. In 1973, Anchor Porter was introduced to the world, a rich, dark beer with a roasted-coffee smell that was unavailable from any of the larger breweries, which were trending toward lighter beers.

Maytag later told the story of the making of that first porter: "I opened the first bag of black malt and was feeding it down into the mill from the floor above. It smelled like espresso coffee, and I thought, 'Oh my God, they sent us coffee instead of black malt!' I'd never brewed with black malt and I didn't know what it was supposed to smell like. It was delicious, the very first brew."

In 1974, with the success of Anchor Porter, the brewery produced seven thousand barrels and made its first profit. Today, they are one of the most successful microbreweries in the United States, producing more than one hundred thousand barrels a year. More important, however, Anchor is given the credit for being the first modern microbrewery in the United States, starting a trend that led to more than 150 microbreweries in the United States in 1994, and a number that is more than double that today. As a successful small brewery, Anchor set the example for all of those that followed to take back the beer market from the major conglomerates and put it back in the historic communities where it started.

Today, Fritz Maytag also operates a California vineyard and manages his family's cheese dairy in Iowa, but the Anchor Brewing Co. has remained his main interest. He is widely regarded as the father of the microbrew movement in the United States.

1967

The Summer of Love

As the tour bus eased onto the crowded street, the passengers could hear the tinny voice of the driver announce through the speakers, "We are now entering the world-famous Haight-Ashbury district." Suddenly, they grabbed their cameras, and crowded the space at the windows. What if they saw someone they knew, or better yet, the child of someone they knew, milling in the streets or peering out of the apartment windows around them.

The fuzzy voice continued above the hum of the engine and the roar of the noise in the street, "We're on Haight Street now and you should look to the left and to the right into the second-story windows. Those are all 'crash pads.' Look! They're naked in there."

Inside the tour bus the passengers in their summer traveling outfits of Bermuda shorts and Madras shirts clicked away with their cameras and peered through their binoculars at the strange sights and sounds all around them on this historic San Francisco street. All around the bus the streets were filled with young men and women with long hair and bare feet, wrapped in blankets, flags, and other bizarre costumes covered with beads and feathers or flowers. Some of the tourists even thought they perceived a faint haze in the air from the burning of marijuana and incense and all around they could smell the musty scent of patchouli oil.

It was the summer of 1967, and the forty blocks known as the Haight-Ashbury district were home to sixteen to twenty thousand self-proclaimed hippies, all blissfully participating in what was known as the Summer of Love. Drugs, such as LSD and marijuana, were certainly a major component of the summer's recipe for peace, love, and freedom to do what you pleased, but the Summer of Love wasn't just about drugs.

In January 1967, ten thousand people had packed into San Francisco's Golden Gate Park to hear former Harvard Professor Timothy Leary speak the words: "Tune in, turn on, drop out." The crowd may not have cheered loudly at the words, but they grooved with them. It was only January, the middle of winter in most places in North America, but it was the beginning of the Summer of Love in San Francisco.

Timothy Leary's message and the hippie movement that flowed from it was a reaction to the strange political climate of the 1960s, and a similar reaction was manifesting itself all over the United States, not just in the area the tour bus companies touted as "the only foreign tour within the continental limits of the U.S." As radical student politics at the

University of California at Berkeley had become the order of the day in the mid-1960s, another breed of student or former student crept quietly onto the scene. While students in black arranged sit-ins, waived placards, and pleaded with passers-by for signatures on petitions for peace in Vietnam and free speech, a new group watched from the fringes of campus. These students, and eventually dropouts, stood out next to their soberly dressed peers, but they made less noise. Long hair, brightly colored tie-dyed T-shirts, feathers, and all manner of strange apparel chose to be an example of what the activists were agitating for—peace.

There were frequent confrontations between the students and police during the campus demonstrations, and many of the students were arrested for their activities. The public in California had also reacted negatively to the agitation on the Berkeley campus. It seemed that the people of California wanted to read about the university on the sports pages of the newspaper and nowhere else. They supported the hard line that officials took against the demonstrators. In fact, part of Ronald Reagan's gubernatorial campaign platform was a vow to reform the University of California and eliminate the demonstrations.

The Summer of Love, and the hippie movement in general, were in part a reaction to the sometimes violent confrontations between the police and activists. While the activists at Berkeley wanted to change the world, the self-proclaimed hippies chose to withdraw from the world, seeing it as essentially degenerate and unlikely to change. Drugs became prevalent at Haight-Ashbury because they helped people tune out the violence in the world around them. At "The Haight" people thought that love was the key element missing in most human relations, and they sought to be an example of what love could do to achieve peace in the world. Many of the former activists at Berkeley dropped their picket signs, grew out their hair, and drifted across the bay to join the free love that filled the summer air.

The problem was that many of the hippies living at the Haight had very little money, food was harder to come by than drugs, and the number of people crowded into the tiny area made for a sanitation nightmare. By the end of the summer, groups of concerned citizens, many looking somewhat like the hippies themselves, had moved in to set up soup kitchens, "safe" houses, and even drug counseling programs.

The Summer of Love was just a brief moment, but its attitudes inspired a generation. Even the busloads of tourists could not fail to be affected when they saw one of the objects of their interest walking alongside the bus holding a mirror for the occupants to see themselves reflected in the activity of the street.

1969

They Chose Alcatraz

There was a scream, the sickening sounds of crashing, then silence. Eight-year-old Yvonne Oakes lay crumpled at the bottom of three flights of stairs at the former prison that had been her home since November 1969. Her father rushed to her side, but there was nothing anyone could do for the girl. It was a bleak moment that crushed the euphoria of the successful take-over of the notorious former federal prison—Alcatraz.

On November 20, 1969, a tiny, glowing light in the distance had let the group of eighty Native Americans know they were on the right track even though the fog kept them from seeing the water just in front of their simple rowboats. Earlier that month, Richard Oakes and four other Native Americans rowed out to Alcatraz Island and put ashore, but they were talked into returning to the mainland the next day. Now, the caretaker at the island welcomed them when they put ashore, claiming he was "Indian, too" and he showed them to the warden's house so that they could use it for shelter.

The group made the following offer to the caretaker, to be shared with the United States government:

> We will give to the inhabitants of this island a portion of that land for their own, to be held in trust by the American Indian Government—for as long as the sun shall rise and the rivers go down to the sea—to be administered by the Bureau of Caucasian Affairs. We will further guide the inhabitants in the proper way of living. We will offer them our religion, our education, our life-ways, in order to help them achieve our level of civilization and thus raise them and all of their white brothers up from their savage and unhappy state.

They further offered to buy the island for "$24 in glass beads and red cloth, a precedent set by the white man's purchase of a similar island about 300 years ago," referring to Peter Stuyvesant's purchase of Manhattan Island from the Native Americans who lived there. It might have been a generous offer. The conditions at the former maximum-security prison on Alcatraz were primitive—there was no plumbing and the heat came from campfires, but they claimed it was still better than most of the Indian Reservations designated for habitation. They were insistent and said, "...we want Alcatraz. We'd accept all of America back if it were possible."

Very few people reacted to their occupation as did California Senator George Murphy. He shuddered, "Somebody's liable to claim the whole U.S." More people supported their efforts and agreed with their position. In fact, many people in San Francisco, including eleven congressmen, supported their efforts and tried to work out a way for them to have other land in exchange for the island.

Other San Francisco residents offered their support in other ways. Student radicals from Berkeley managed to evade the Coast Guard in small boats and toss fruit, vegetables, beer, milk, and two turkeys onto shore. By Thanksgiving, there were 300 Native Americans on the island and the Bratskellar restaurant in San Francisco provided their dinner. They sent twenty turkeys, cranberry sauce, sweet potatoes, and cake.

In December 1969, the group gathered on the island announced they were there to stay. One hundred fifty became permanent residents in a special ceremony, while one hundred eighty-three visitors witnessed the formation of an island government. The flag the group chose to represent this government had a broken peace pipe and a crimson teepee on a blue background.

The United States government had been trying to sell Alcatraz Island and its prison for five years, ever since the prison had closed in 1963. A few developers showed some interest, including one man who wanted to turn the island and its prison into an upscale shopping area filled with fancy boutiques. But because of its remote location and forbidding appearance, two things that made for an ideal prison location, no one pursued their interest in commercial development very far. In fact, before the 1969 Native American occupation, four other groups had taken over the island and occupied it since the prison's closing. All had given up after just a short time of dealing with the lack of fresh water and heat at the crumbling prison site.

This time, it was different, though. The federal government tried to ignore the group, thinking they, too, would give up. In addition, officials were nervous about trying to remove the group that was claiming Alcatraz Island forcibly. There was simply too much public support for the small group—and the group was becoming larger every day. Eventually, the Army Corps of Engineers was authorized to park a barge off the island to provide for the group's fresh-water needs.

As the word spread about the apparent success of the group on Alcatraz, similar take-overs were staged all over the United States—at Fort Lawton in Seattle, at Ellis Island in New York Harbor, and at Rattlesnake Island in California's Clear Lake. These groups claimed unoccupied federal land as their own under a provision in an old Sioux treaty that said Indians could occupy it if it was unused by the government.

When these other groups began to copy the invasion of Alcatraz, the government changed its mind about its policy. The occupants of the island announced May 31 as the deadline to turn the area over to them permanently, and the government responded by announcing that the area would become part of a Bay Area national park. Shortly thereafter, the government removed the water barge and cut off electricity to the island.

There was carefully planned symbolism involved in the decision to take over Alcatraz, the former prison, and to claim it as Indian Territory. Many of those involved believed that Indian Reservations were mere prisoner-of-war camps, so it was ironic that they would choose the infamous former prison as the place to make their statement. In addition, with the further deprivations caused by the removal of water and the cutting off of electricity, the island became even more bleak, perhaps, than it had been for the prisoners who had been detained there in earlier days.

Eventually, time and hardship took their toll. The group had dwindled from an all-time high of three hundred residents to a low of twenty-five to thirty. Among those who had gone from the island was Richard Oakes, the father of the little girl killed in the fall, who was one of the spokesmen for the group and a fine leader. In ensuing months, the little group became smaller and began to fall apart.

Finally, in June 1971, U.S. troops removed the few remaining stragglers from their stronghold on the island. It had been a valiant effort on the part of the small group, and it was an essential part of the American Indian movement of the 1970s because of the attention brought to the Indian's plight and the support it garnered from the public.

1975

The Homebrew Computer Club

The cover of the January 1975 issue of *Popular Mechanics* got Gordon French and Fred Moore thinking. The magazine was introducing a new kit—the Altair—that you could buy to build your own personal computer. The computer wasn't much, just a circuit board and some connections, but it had new and exciting possibilities for engineers who were interested in personal computing in the mid-1970s. Among other things, it wasn't the size of a refrigerator—and it was relatively affordable. Here was a new way for people interested in computers to start thinking about them differently.

The computer industry had deep roots in the region of California where Menlo Park could be found already. Hewlett-Packard got its start in a Palo Alto garage in 1939, starting an era of computing in the area that would come to be known as Silicon Valley—but all over the world, electrical engineers and scientists were working to create the first massive computer systems, machines that occupied entire rooms and operated using vacuum tube technology. By the time French and Moore saw the Altair on the front cover of *Popular Mechanics*, people had been talking for years about new technology that would streamline operations and make computers both more portable and more affordable. Hewlett-Packard had been making enormous strides in the area of personal computing, employing many of the most talented engineers in the area. A revolution was about to start.

French and Moore's idea for what they called the Homebrew Computer Club was simple. They would start a club for people like them who were interested in computers and their potential. So they handed out flyers inviting people with "like-minded interests" to a meeting in Moore's garage on March 5, 1975. One of the fliers ended up on the bulletin board at Hewlett-Packard, where two young employees named Alan Baum and Steve Wozniak spotted it. Baum and Wozniak made it to the meeting—where Wozniak saw a specification sheet for a microprocessor and saw a demonstration of the kit that everyone was talking about. Wozniak had a crazy idea. What if the circuits and the microprocessor and even a keyboard and a screen could all be integrated into a new kind of personal computer?

Hewlett Packard was already making personal computers that were becoming more common in industry and in university settings—but Wozniak thought he could do better. He started working at his regular job during the day, buying all the parts he could find through his connections in the industry, and then working tirelessly at night to build his own computer. On June 29, 1975, he made a major breakthrough. He typed some letters on his keyboard and they appeared on the screen in front of him that he'd designed to work in concert with the computer. He later said, "It was the first time in history anyone had typed a character on a keyboard and seen it shown up on their own computer's screen right in front of them."

When Wozniak showed his invention to his good friend Steve Jobs, Jobs was very impressed and almost immediately grasped the potential of the new device. Wozniak and Jobs had known each other since 1971, when Jobs was still a high school student. The two had quickly bonded over their shared interest in pranks—and their interest in electrical engineering and the possibilities of home computers. Once Wozniak had demonstrated what might be done using the new microprocessors, as they called them, the two banded together to develop a product that they could potentially sell to customers. Jobs started going to the Homebrew meetings with Wozniak and sourcing parts for him as they worked to improve the product, which they called the Apple I. The two sold fifty of the fully assembled computers to a store called the Byte Shop.

Wozniak was happy with the Apple I, but he was sure they could do even better. With the money they earned from the Apple I, he started work on the Apple II, which had a case and a keyboard and a text display that had the option of color, as well as a way to store programs and data on disks. Jobs and Wozniak formed a company, got a loan from a bank, and built more of the new, better personal computers. They first showed the Apple II to the public in April 1977. It was an immediate success.

Nearly eight years later, football fans all over America were settled into living rooms and rec rooms littered with pizza boxes and chip-and-dip bowls on January 22, 1984, watching the Los Angeles Raiders defeat the Washington Redskins in Super Bowl XVIII when, during the third quarter, something amazing happened. Super Bowl ads were expensive and the companies that chose to advertise during the game usually played it safe. People were watching the game, not the commercials. They were refilling the chips during the commercials. Then something incredible happened.

On screen, rows of bald men in baggy gray clothes marched in time to seats in front of a television screen featuring a man spouting ideology in a scene taken from George Orwell's famous novel *1984*, which envisioned a homogenous, highly structured world controlled by the totalitarian "Big Brother," who would appear on television screens. As the men march, a blond woman in red shorts wielding a sledgehammer runs toward the gigantic screen and flings it into the face, destroying the message. On the screen the words read:

On January 24, Apple Computer will introduce Macintosh. And you'll see why 1984 won't be like "1984."

Today, almost everyone watches the ads during the Super Bowl, and almost no one uses a Macintosh. But the 1985 Macintosh ad started a revolution in Super Bowl advertising and the Macintosh started a revolution in personal computers. Now everyone knows the iPod and the iPad and the Apple Watch and the MacBook—all because the Homebrew Computer Club started a revolution back in that garage in 1975.

1976

Christo's Running Fence

Everett Winkelman of Petaluma, California, had to laugh as he counted the money from his sale. He'd sold forty-two of these 18-by-25-foot panels of white nylon curtain—some for more than sixty dollars. People even liked them better when they had burrs stuck in them or snags and rusty spots. "I could have sold a couple hundred if I'd had that many. People have come from all over the country asking for them," he said.

Winkelman was only one of the many residents of Northern California's central valley who had recently become an entrepreneur. People all over Marin and Sonoma counties were selling fragments of this nylon cloth to tourists—or using them for windbreaks, hay caps, bedspreads, and shower curtains. One person even made a raincoat and hat from the white fabric.

The nylon had come from a very unusual art project that was in place for only two weeks in September 1976. A forty-one-year-old artist from Bulgaria named Christo Javacheff, but who went only by Christo, had erected a 18-foot-high, white nylon fence that zig-zagged for 24.5 miles through the rolling hills of Northern California's Sonoma and Marin counties. The whole project had cost more than three million dollars—and before Christo could build it, he had to get permission from the landowners whose property it would cross.

Previously, Christo had gift-wrapped a mile-and-a-half section of cliff in Australia and in 1972 had hung an orange piece called "Valley Curtain" from mountain to mountain across the highway at Riffle Gap, Colorado, but his work was relatively unknown in this predominantly farming community. The locals were skeptical about this artist and his crazy idea, and it took seventeen public hearings and three court sessions for him to gain permission from the counties the fence would pass through.

Still, Christo wanted to build his fence in spite of, or even because of, any difficulties he might have in getting it built. He believed that the process of creating the work was just as much art as the final piece itself would be. He waited patiently while a 450-page environmental impact report was compiled and written, and then he sat patiently during the many hearings, meetings, and protests until the work could be started. It took more than forty-two months, and fifty-nine ranchers had to agree to lease their land to Christo before he could erect the fence.

A local committee of artists, called the "Committee to Stop the Fence," protested loudly and long against the project. They didn't consider what Christo was doing art, and they wanted it stopped. But many people in the art world had positive things to say about Christo's fence once it was standing. It was described by some as "beautiful, amazing" as it passed through the high, nearly treeless hills where cattle roamed peacefully through a rainless summer. One critic spoke of the fence as a living thing and said, "Sometimes the Fence would vanish behind a hill and suddenly reappear miles farther along the road; then you knew it had been following you all the while."

In spite of all the effort and reports, good reviews and bad, the fence still caused controversy during its two-week existence, from September 8 to September 22, 1976. In fact, part of the fence may have been illegal, as it crossed too close to protected shoreline.

Once the fence came down, though, many people decided it was worth all the fuss. This crazy project had created jobs, caused a short-lived tourist boom, and fostered community pride. Sonoma County even designated the spot where the fence had crossed Highway 101 a local historical landmark. Local restaurants and motels benefited immediately from the stir Christo's fence caused, and from the labor required to put it all together.

The building of the fence was a massive effort. It took thousands of people to create the materials and put them together. The fence itself was made up of 2,050 panels of the white cloth, each 18 feet high and 68 feet wide, and 2,050 steel poles, each 21 feet high and buried 3 feet in the ground, formed the structure. Ninety miles of steel cable and 312,000 steel hooks held the whole thing together. Students were paid $2.50 an hour to assemble and later disassemble the structure. A factory in West Virginia had been hired to weave the 165,000 yards of white nylon cloth. Had the factory not gotten the contract, it might have shut down, because its contract for making parachutes for the Army had just run out.

Once the two weeks of the fence's existence were over, it took almost a month to dismantle the whole thing. It was the dismantling that spurred a strange cottage industry in the sleepy central-California valley. The parts of the fence, including the 2,050 steel poles and all the yards of cloth, were distributed among the landowners whose property the work of art had crossed. The poles were divided up and used for fence posts and the fabric unused by the property holders was sold either directly to the public or to local entrepreneurs. The tourists who bought the fabric—many of whom would frame their fragments and hang them on the wall, much to the entertainment of the locals using them in the barnyard—amazed the sellers.

Ed Pozzi, a farmer in Valley Ford, said, "We always thought Christo was kind of weird, but not anymore. He provided employment for a lot of people, and we got a few dollars out of it, too. We all miss it. I don't suppose we'll ever see anything like it again."

Pozzi kept his pieces of Christo's fence. He thought they might really be worth something someday.

1978

Harvey Milk and George Moscone Murdered

At almost eleven o'clock on the morning of November 27, 1978, Cyr Copertini, San Francisco Mayor George Moscone's secretary, heard what sounded like a car backfiring in the street outside of city hall. Copertini went to the window to look for the car but didn't see anything. Seconds later, Deputy Mayor Rudy Nothemburg, who had also heard the noise and had seen someone running from the other entrance to the mayor's private office, stepped inside and saw the blood on the floor where the forty-nine-year-old mayor lay. He had been shot four times—twice in the body and twice in the head.

Nothemburg ran out of the office and with Copertini alerted the rest of the building. A few minutes later, the body of city supervisor Harvey Milk was found near his office—riddled with five bullet holes.

Ordinarily, security at San Francisco's city hall was tight. All employees had to pass through an electronic checkpoint at the entrance to the building, where security guards would be aware of any weapons that entered the building. As a former city supervisor, however, Dan White was able to get a building employee to let him in through another door. He had quarreled briefly with Moscone in his office before shooting him and had then gone after another city supervisor, Harvey Milk.

At ten-thirty that morning, Mayor George Moscone had reluctantly told his secretary that he would meet with Dan White. White had resigned his position earlier that month, claiming the salary was too low, but then he had second thoughts. He had previously contacted Moscone and asked for his job back. Moscone was ready to appoint his replacement and didn't want to continue the argument, but he invited White in for a conversation.

Moscone's refusal to reappoint White after his resignation was the obvious reason for White's anger, but there was another issue at stake for the angry ex-supervisor. Forty-eight-year-old Harvey Milk was the first out-of-the-closet gay man to serve in high public office in San Francisco. In addition, he was an official who campaigned for gay rights with the support of Mayor Moscone. In San Francisco, where gays made up approximately fifteen percent of the total population and had unprecedented influence over city government, White, a conservative who opposed gay rights, was in the minority among the city officials—most of whom supported San Francisco's reputation as the "town that tolerates everything."

San Francisco had been a city of great diversity since its earliest days, and in the 1970s, the trend had continued.

Only one in three people in the city were white, third-generation American citizens. Blacks, Hispanics, Chinese, Japanese, Filipinos, and Samoans made up more than 40 percent of the voters in the city. It was surprising that White, a thirty-two-year-old ex-fireman, had even been elected. Once he was on the board, he stood in direct opposition to everything Harvey Milk stood for.

In fact, White had cast the only negative vote on the board against San Francisco's landmark homosexual-rights ordinance, and then had taken his loss badly. A colleague was heard to say of White after the loss, "He showed no sense of humor, fair play, or sportsmanship." White believed that he stood for everything that was right with America and that Milk was a pervert who had no business participating in politics.

During the afternoon and evening following the double murder, the city of San Francisco mourned its mayor and city supervisor. Red roses tied with black bows and other remembrances were placed on city hall's steps as the word spread through town. That night, four drummers beat a solemn rhythm as 25,000 citizen mourners marched behind them up Market Street to the civic center where folk singer Joan Baez led the crowd in hymns.

Acting Mayor Dianne Feinstein spoke eloquently of the lives of Moscone and Milk and of the compassion shown by the city saying, "In our sorrow, this lovely jewel of a city seems a dark and saddened place. Let us build together, for the San Francisco we all love."

But the most poignant moment of the night was yet to come. Harvey Milk had left a tape recording with a friend to be played in case of his assassination. In it he said, "I hope that every professional gay [will] just say, 'Enough!' come forward, and tell everybody. Wear a sign, let the world know. Maybe that will help."

In all the confusion after the shootings, Dan White was actually able to slip out of city hall undetected after borrowing an aide's car. He met his wife at St. Mary's Cathedral and they walked together to the police station where White confessed to the murders. He had shot both Mayor Moscone and Harvey Milk with a snub-nosed .38.

The reason White gave for the murders was the obvious one. He was upset because Moscone wouldn't reappoint him to the board of supervisors after his resignation, and because Milk supported Moscone's decision. He had argued with Moscone over the decision, killed him, and then gone on to continue the argument with Milk. People all over San Francisco believed, however, that it wouldn't have come to murder had Milk not been gay.

Having confessed to the murders, Dan White faced a strange irony. In November, Moscone and Milk—both strong opponents of capital punishment—had fought a ballot initiative that expanded the death penalty in California. They were unsuccessful in stopping the bill, which, among other things, made it a capital offense to murder a public official in pursuit of his duties. White, who had been an outspoken supporter of the measure, would now have to face the possibility of execution himself.

Eventually, White was convicted of voluntary manslaughter after a controversial court case. To the outrage of many people familiar with the case, he was imprisoned for a few years, then returned to a still-hostile San Francisco. On October 21, 1985, he took his own life.

1987

Harmony on Mount Shasta

It was late on Friday night, August 14, when Diane Boettcher, a resident of Mount Shasta City, turned on her television to watch the news. She had just settled in to catch up on the day's events when suddenly the fuzzy image of an angel appeared on the screen along with the anchor who was calmly reading the news. Startled, she switched channels, but the angel remained. Then she unplugged the cable—and it was still on the screen.

The next day, the television repairman was there to check it out, but all he could say was, "It looks like you've got an angel on your screen." Then, apparently, he went off to contemplate the meaning of it all.

As word of the appearance spread, people flocked to Diane's house hoping for a glimpse of the mysterious angel.

Diane remained unconcerned about the masses of people who appeared. She said, "It doesn't really matter if it's real or not, because it's made these people happy."

What made the appearance of the "angel" in the television even more remarkable was the time it chose to make its appearance. According to some "new age" philosophers, August 16, 1987 was to be the time of the "harmonic convergence," a time when the dead would be raised, UFOs would land, devastating earthquakes would cover the Earth, Quetzalcoatl the Aztec god would reveal himself, and the world would end. August 16 was supposed to be the day when the planets would be in rare alignment and the 5,125-year-old Mayan calendar would finally end.

Three hundred fifty "sacred sites" had been identified throughout the United States, where believers in the harmonic convergence could gather to create a human power grid to set the world at rights, or at least to watch from great seats what was about to happen. The idea was the brainchild of Jose Arguelles, a forty-eight-year-old artist and historian from Boulder, Colorado, whose book, *The Mayan Factor*, which explained the theory of convergence, was the start of the uproar. Thousands gathered on Ohio's Great Serpent Mound, at New York's Niagara Falls, Woodstock, and Central Park, and around the world people gathered at Stonehenge, Machu Picchu, and the Great Pyramids. The general atmosphere of the gatherings was very Woodstock-esque, with handholding, hugging, and the eerie sound of meditative hums the order of the day.

About five thousand people had converged on Mount Shasta for the harmonizing, and many of those visited the home of Diane Boettcher to see the angel. Diane, herself a theosophist planning to attend the Sunday morning event, had plenty of crystals arranged around the TV for maximum energy.

On Sunday morning, August 16, at 5:00 a.m. Eastern Time, the convergers began congregating in their designated spots. On Mount Shasta, the five thousand sat shivering in the pre-dawn chill, waiting for the sun to warm the fir-covered rocky slopes. Before the sun rose, the sounds of drums and flutes filled the air, and people began their yoga, meditation, and harmonizing.

Jose Arguelles claimed the cause for the convergence was three planets—Mars, Mercury, and Venus—which would line up with the new moon. This would cause, he said, according to the ancient Mayan Indian calendar, the material world to cease existence unless 144,000 people would gather at the sacred sites and meditate to bring on a new age of peace and harmony.

It was unclear whether the 144,000 souls needed to avert disaster according to Arguelles actually did show up that weekend. At many of the "sacred sites" the turnout was much lower than expected, but that didn't deter the hardy few who did show up. But the world didn't end, and none of the prophesied events—from the return of Aztec gods to the earthquakes rocking the planet—took place.

As for Diane Boettcher's angel, it stayed in her television, and no one seemed to know what to do to remove it, but it didn't spout any divine wisdom about the end of the world. The planets did align as expected, but Dr. William Gooch of the Hayden Planetarium in Manhattan explained that. He reassured an only slightly concerned general public that planets align all the time, and that there was no mystery to the combination. He said, "As far as science is concerned, there is absolutely nothing unusual about the day. Events like this happen quite regularly. It just depends on which group of planets you choose to pick. The only cycle I see is that a lot of people want to get back to hippie days."

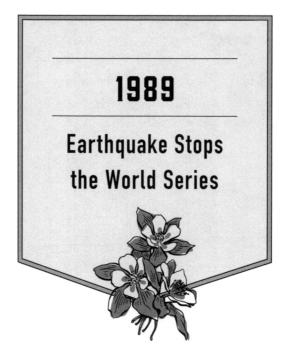

1989

Earthquake Stops the World Series

When the shaking started, the players in the locker rooms just thought beer kegs were being rolled down the concrete ramps over their heads. Sportscasters in the press box watched as the TV monitors mounted in front of them swayed gently back and forth like cobras emerging from a snake charmer's basket. As the stadium rocked, chunks of concrete fell off its massive walls, one landing in a seat a man had just vacated in search of a hot dog, but no one suffered much of an injury. When it stopped, sportscaster Peter Gammons calmly told the person next to him that this one was a 5.4 tops—referring to the quake's magnitude on the Richter scale—not a big one at all. Several people in the stands yelled, "Play Ball!" ready for the game to begin immediately; a fan hastily constructed a sign that read "That was nothing. Wait till the Giants bat!"

Sixty thousand people were in the concrete stadium on Candlestick Point near San Francisco waiting for the start of Game 3 of the 1989 World Series between the Oakland A's and the San Francisco Giants. The series was a dream come true for Bay Area baseball fans. This was their chance to see all seven games of the greatest sporting event of the year right in their own backyards, as both Bay Area teams battled for the title of World Champion.

The weather was absolutely perfect for the series, and people kept commenting on it. The summer storms that winds usually carried into the Bay Area from the Pacific were over, the skies were clear, and the weather was warm, even balmy. Only a few people were around who remembered that the weather had been much the same in April 1906 before the great earthquake and fire razed the city of San Francisco; fewer dared to suggest that the mild October days suggested earthquake weather.

The crowd at the stadium had been looking forward to a fine game on that beautiful October afternoon, and they had no reason to suspect the earth was about to shake; the weather actually had nothing to do with it, and there was no way of predicting how big or bad this one would be. The A's were ahead in the series two games to one, but Giants fans were confident that the home-field advantage of Candlestick Park would propel the team into a series win.

Within a few minutes of the last shake of the massive stadium, regardless of how excited the fans were to begin the game and unexcited they were about the quake, the police cleared the seats. The crowd, which had just been tossed about in a concrete bowl more than one hundred feet above the shaking ground, left quietly. The game couldn't go on that night; the loudspeakers and scoreboards weren't working. No one in the stadium knew how devastating the quake had actually been outside its walls in the Bay Area.

Outside of Candlestick Park, parts of San Francisco were in ruins. The Marina District, an upper-middle-class neighborhood, was the hardest hit. Bob Welch, the only member of either the Oakland A's or the San Francisco Giants who actually lived in San Francisco, had been in the training room when the quake started; when he realized what it was, he feared the worst. He and his wife had just bought a new house in the Marina District. They planned to move in two weeks, after the series. Now, with the game canceled, he drove home to see how bad it had been. Once there, he joined the crowd of other residents who were not allowed to get in to inspect the damage. The next day they could go to a local middle school and apply for permission to visit their homes. Many people would receive red tickets from the city indicating that their houses would have to be torn down. No one was above the need for the special entry permit. Joe DiMaggio, the great former New York Yankee, stood in line just like Bob Welch of the Giants and everyone else.

The timing of the quake—just as commuters were headed home for the night—could not have been worse. At the Bay Bridge, part of the top tier had collapsed, trapping drivers and their cars above San Francisco Bay. More devastating was the downward crash of the Cypress Street Viaduct of the Nimitz Freeway. Authorities estimated that more than 250 people were trapped and probably crushed when the concrete roadway gave way. More than $10 billion in damages had happened just outside Candlestick Park while the stadium rocked and swayed.

The ironic part was that no one in San Francisco, not just the fans who were at the World Series Game 3, knew how bad the quake was until much later. Power was out all over the city; people were getting their information on the streets and from battery-powered radios that could pick up stations in areas unaffected by the quake. But because an estimated sixty million baseball fans in the United States and millions more around the world were tuned in to watch the game when the quake hit, they all knew the story of the San Francisco earthquake as it happened.

Amazingly, what could have been a greater tragedy for San Francisco, as well as for the game of baseball had Candlestick Park not withstood the quake so well, was not as bad as it could have been precisely because of the game. The death toll on the Nimitz highway was not in the hundreds as was originally thought; fewer people were on their way home at their usual hour because they had left work early to tune in to the World Series game. It was the same at the Bay Bridge. People all over were at home, tuned into the game, and not in the streets. In fact, fewer than one hundred people made their way to San Francisco General Hospital and Highland Hospital in Oakland the night of the quake with related injuries.

The morning after the shake-up, newly appointed Baseball Commissioner Fay Vincent held a press conference lit by candlelight—the power was still out. Game 3 of the World Series, "our modest little sporting event," as Vincent called it, was postponed, but it would not leave the Bay Area. The teams remained to play out their games—eventually—and their advertisers supported the decision. Both groups would help extensively with relief efforts in the city.

The day before the earthquake, sportswriter Tom Gage of the *Detroit News* made the following comment in his column.

> After two losses, the Giants are down to their secret weapon: Earthquake. . . . Barring seismographic activity which would render Candlestick Park and alternate sites inaccessible before resumption of the World Series on Tuesday, the Giants are in serious trouble. They need more time to figure out how to beat the confident A's.

Tom Gage could never have imagined how prophetic his words would be, but the extra time was still not enough for the Giants to make a comeback. Eventually, the Giants would lose to the A's, four games to zero, with the final game held on October 28, just eleven days after the earthquake struck. More was made of the earthquake than of any player's performance, and the games were played simply and without fanfare, as if both teams realized they were playing in a "modest little sporting event" against the backdrop of a great tragedy. It just happened that the sporting event was important enough to so many people that it may have kept the tragedy from being worse.

2020

The August Complex Fire

It was summer in Northern California, a place where inland temperatures generally soared into the nineties during the day, but cool evenings would bring friends and neighbors out onto decks and patios, greeting each other from yard to yard, sharing a toast and enjoying socially distanced evenings while enjoying a bit of what had brought many of them to the forested areas of the state. The scenery, the beautiful weather, the space for chickens and rescue horses and dogs—all were part of the California dream. They were the things that kept long-time residents there and that drew newcomers from around the world.

California had been hit hard by the worldwide coronavirus pandemic, along with the rest of the United States. Some of the first cases of the disease had appeared in California—as early as January 2020. Individual counties began canceling large group gatherings, closing schools, and shuttering restaurants and bars and amusement parks. Governor Gavin Newsom moved quickly to shut down businesses and schools on a statewide basis and to impose stay-at-home orders to try to stop the spread of disease through the country's largest state. In populated areas, the fear was that the highly transmittable virus would "spread like wildfire."

For many people around the U.S., who had also been staying at home, the coming of warm spring and summer months was a relief after weeks of shutdown. In California, especially in the rural farming and ranching communities, a lot of life went on business as usual. Livestock had to be tended, fences needed maintenance, and warm summer temperatures meant even more time outside—enjoying hiking and biking and fishing and other safe outdoor pursuits.

Over the last few decades, however, Northern California had been getting warmer in the summer. And the usually dry climate became drier still. Forest management practices had led to an increase in the amount of fuel available in its densely forested areas. And development had led to an increasing number of people building homes and businesses in areas that were potential forest-fire zones. One transplanted resident from the Midwest would later say that "no one ever suggested that wildfires made the move a bad idea." Sure, forest fires happened in California, and Oregon, and Washington, and Idaho, and Montana. But they were part of the package along with earthquakes and average snowfall. Still, when the whole town of Paradise, California, burned in 2018, displacing thousands of residents in one of California's biggest forest-fire disasters ever, more people began to prepare for the worst. Just a single spark could start a major conflagration and give residents little warning.

On August 16 and 17, 2020, thunderstorms moved inland from a tropical storm over the Pacific Ocean, causing lightning strikes in Mendocino and Glenn counties and starting small fires. On August 17, a hundred-acre fire near the town of Willows had a name, and it had firefighters in place working to extinguish the blaze. The Doe Fire, as it was called, had yet to be contained, and other fires—the Elkhorn, the Hopkins, the Box, and more—were erupting as crews arrived to contain them.

There were so many fires popping up so quickly, and so many teams on the ground and in the air involved in the effort to contain them, that the Forest Service made the decision to name them the "August Complex." By the morning of August 20, the first grouped under that name had burned 65,000 acres. Four days later, that number would double as fires grew and whole areas, already superheated from the years of warmer temperatures and full of dry tinder, caught and burned.

The fires were moving faster and growing larger than they ever had before. Fire managers and forestry scientists were alarmed because they were having difficulty giving adequate warning to residents about the path of the blazes and how quickly they might reach an inhabited area. A professor at Syracuse University who studies the environment and wildfires said, "We have seen multiple fires expand by tens of thousands of acres in a matter of hours, and thirty years or more ago, that was just not fire behavior that we saw." The fires, caused by storms, were spreading like wildfire. And the smoke and ash as far away as Montana and Wyoming were driving residents into their homes as air quality declined throughout the West.

Over the next two months, evacuation orders were issued and rescinded throughout the counties affected by the flames. Neighbors welcomed neighbors despite the conditions of the ongoing pandemic as homes and businesses burned. In September, firefighting teams were spread out over Trinity County and toward Humboldt County and still hard at work trying to contain the blazes in Mendocino and Glenn. Lake, Trinity, Tehama, and Shasta counties would soon be part of the affected area and part of the struggle to quench the flames.

By the end of September, when students should have been back in classrooms and the first signs of fall should have been evident in the trees, the closures caused by the pandemic were still in effect, the evacuations due to fire were still ongoing, the air quality outdoors was still considered unhealthy, and the August Complex fire, which had grown to more than 900,000 acres, was still only 43 percent contained. The end was not yet in sight.

October should have brought rains to California—but in October, the change in weather was still slow in coming. A "la Nina" climate event over the Pacific was keeping the air dry and warm. October 5 was a major milestone for the August Complex—the total area of the fires was measured at just over a million acres. It was officially the first "giga" fire in California history. And it had eclipsed all previous fires, becoming the largest in state history. One firefighter had been killed, almost a thousand structures had been lost or were damaged, and untold damage had been done to those exposed to the smoke and possibly even to the groundwater in the area. It was a disaster of massive proportions.

The weather finally changed, as weather does, and on November 9, as cooler temperatures and moisture moved across the region, fire managers were able to report that the blaze was 95 percent contained. Three days later the crisis was declared "over" and the teams disbanded as the area's residents went about rebuilding or deciding whether to rebuild. The fire in Northern California was out—for now.

The pandemic continued to keep Californians at home, but good news was on the horizon as vaccines were deployed and restrictions lifted. But, like the threat from global pandemics, the threat from wildfire is also not over. For Californians, forest fire has always been part of life in the Golden State, and it always will be.

A POTPOURRI OF NORTHERN CALIFORNIA FACTS

The name California first appeared in a Romantic novel, published in Seville, Spain, in about 1510. The book, *Las Sergas de Esplandián*, by Garcí Rodríguez Ordóñez de Montalvo described a fantastic, mythical island called California, and the Spanish adopted the name for the land to the north of their conquests in South America.

Between 1860 and 1960 the population of California nearly doubled every twenty years.

According to the official U.S. 2020 census, 39,538,223 people now live in California, which is the most populous state.

California comprises 158,693 square miles, spans ten degrees of latitude, and has 1,264 miles of coast. It is the third largest state, after Alaska and Texas.

California experiences about five thousand earthquakes every year, but most of them are so small that only seismologists know they occur.

The Sierra Nevada receives thirty to forty feet of snowfall in average years, and in peak years as much as sixty feet fall in the mountains.

There were between 150,000 and 300,000 Native Americans living in California when the Spanish first arrived. That's four times the density of the population of any other aboriginal population in what is now the United States.

The Native Americans who were the first human inhabitants of California developed more than one hundred dialects in several different language families.

California's state motto is "Eureka!" which means, "I have found it!"

At 14,496 feet, Mount Whitney is the tallest mountain in the contiguous forty-eight states.

Death Valley is the lowest point in the United States at an average 279.6 feet below sea level. The lowest point in Death Valley is Badwater at 282 feet below sea level.

California's capital is Sacramento.

California's nickname is the "Golden State," a reminder of the 1848 discovery of gold in the state. Other "gold" California icons are the golden poppy and California's state fish, the golden trout.

California's state bird is the California valley quail.

The state tree is the California Redwood.

California is first in the United States in total farm income. Crops raised in the state make up more than 10 percent of the total farm income of the United States.

From 1848 to 1857, California gold fields produced $370,000,000 or an average of $41,000,000 per year.

In the mid-1870s, California had about the same size population as the state of Connecticut, but the residents spent nearly six times as much as Connecticut did on public schools. Today, the state still spends more on education than any other state.

California's professional sports teams have won multiple major championships in basketball, football, and baseball, but it wasn't until 2012 that a California team (the Los Angeles Kings) finally won hockey's Stanley Cup. The Kings won the championship a second time in 2014.

BIBLIOGRAPHY

BOOKS

Alcatraz Is Not an Island. Berkeley, California: Wingbow Press, 1972.

Bauer, Helen. *California Indian Days.* Garden City, New York: Doubleday, 1968.

Bosworth, Alan R. *America's Concentration Camps.* New York: W.W. Norton, 1967.

Bronson, William. *The Earth Shook, The Sky Burned.* Garden City, New York: Doubleday, 1959.

Davis, Daniel S. *Behind Barbed Wire: The Imprisonment of Japanese Americans during World War II.* New York: E. P. Dutton, 1982.

Egan, Ferol. *Frémont: Explorer for a Restless Nation.* Garden City, New York: Doubleday, 1977.

Dillon, Richard. *Burnt-Out Fires: California's Modoc Indian War.* Englewood Cliffs, New Jersey: Prentice Hall, 1973.

Garst, Shannon. *Jack London: Magnet for Adventure.* New York: Julian Messner, 1944.

Goldberg, George. *East Meets West: The Story of the Chinese and Japanese in California.* New York: Harcourt, Brace, Jovanovich, 1970.

Hansen, Gladys, and Emmet Condon. *Denial of Disaster.* San Francisco: Cameron and Co., 1989.

BIBLIOGRAPHY

Hart, James D. *Companion to California*. Berkeley: University of California Press, 1987.

Hutchinson, W. H. *California: Two Centuries of Man, Land, and Growth in the Golden State*. Palo Alto, California: American West Publishing Co., 1969.

Kroeber, Theodora. *Ishi in Two Worlds: A Biography of the Last Wild Indian in North America*. Berkeley: University of California Press, 1961.

Lavender, David Sievert. *Snowbound: The Tragic Story of the Donner Party*. New York: Holiday House, 1996.

Longstreet, Stephen. *The Wilder Shore: A History of the Gala Days of San Francisco*. Garden City, New York: Doubleday, 1968.

McGinty, Brian. *Strong Wine: The Life and Legend of Agoston Haraszthy*. Stanford: Stanford University Press, 1998.

Morrison, Dorothy N. *Under a Strong Wind: The Adventures of Jessie Benton Frémont*. New York: Athenum, 1983.

Rawls, James J. *Indians of California: The Changing Image*. Norman: University of Oklahoma Press, 1984.

Roske, Ralph J. *Everyman's Eden: A History of California*. New York: Macmillan, 1968.

Sarasohn, Eileen Sunada. *Issei Women: Echoes from Another Frontier*. Palo Alto, California: Pacific Books, 1998.

Stone, Irving. *Sailor on Horseback*. Boston: Houghton-Mifflin, 1938.

Thomas, Gordon, and Max Morgan Witts. *The San Francisco Earthquake*. New York: Stein and Day, 1971.

Uchida, Yoshiko. *The Invisible Thread*. Englewood Cliffs, New Jersey: Julian Messner, 1991.

MAGAZINE AND NEWSPAPER ARTICLES

"A Fence to Remember." *Newsweek*. February 21, 1977.

"A Man in Command." *Sports Illustrated*. October 30, 1989.

"Anomie at Alcatraz." *Time*. April 12, 1971.

Bennet, Jr., Lerone. "The Mystery of Mary Ellen Pleasant." *Ebony*. May 1979.

Brooks, Christopher. "The Birth of the Microbrews…" *Country Living*. October 1, 1995.

BIBLIOGRAPHY

"Day of the Assassin." *Newsweek.* December 11, 1978.

"Earthquake." *Time.* October 30, 1989.

Frankenstein, Alfred. "Report from California—Christo's 'Fence' Beauty or Betrayal?" *Art in America.* November 1976.

Friedman, Jack. "Up Front: Hum if You Love the Mayans." *People.* August 31, 1987.

Friedrich, Otto. "New Age Harmonies: A Strange Mix of Spirituality and Superstition Is Sweeping across the Country." *Time.* December 7, 1987.

"Golden Gate Bridge," Office of Historic Preservation, California State Parks.

"He Brought the Olympics to Squaw Valley." *Reader's Digest.* February 1960.

Hill, Evan. "California's Olympic Bonanza." *Saturday Evening Post.* February 13, 1960.

History on this Day, May 17, 1937, "Golden Gate Bridge Opens," https://www.history.com/this-day-in-history/golden-gate-bridge-opens

www.goldengate.org

"Leathernecks Take On an Unusual Foe at Olympic Site." *Life.* February 15, 1960.

Lewis, Kathy. "Candlelight Vigil Honors Memory of Indian Island Massacre." *The Circle.* April 30, 1995.

Morris, Ian, "How We Escaped the Worst of the California Wildfires," *The New Yorker*, 9/22/2020.

"New Flag over Alcatraz." *Time.* January 5, 1970.

New York Times, 4/22/2020.

"None but the Brave." *Newsweek.* July 6, 1970.

Olsen, Bobbi. "Weekend Escape: San Jose; Guns and Roses; A Bit of Supernatural Mystery, Intrigue, and Lots of Night Magic in a Town Everyone Knows the Way To." *Los Angeles Times.* October 6, 1996.

"On to Squaw Valley." *Newsweek.* February 9, 1959.

Sacramento Bee, 9/10/2020.

Skube, Michael. "MS on Beer: Ace Brewmaster Anchors Conference." *Atlanta Journal and Constitution.* March 26, 1998.

BIBLIOGRAPHY

Smilgis, Martha. "Living: A New Age Dawning Oommm . . . Around the World." *Time.* August 31, 1987.

"The Birds II." *Discover.* November 1, 1995.

"The Day the World Series Stopped." *Sports Illustrated.* October 30, 1989.

"Their Ride of Terror." *Sports Illustrated.* October 30, 1989.

"'There was no fighting this fire,' California Survivor Says." AP News Story, 9/11/2020.

USA Today, September 10, 2020.

Thompson, Hunter S. "The Hashbury Is the Capital of the Hippies." *The New York Times Magazine.* May 14, 1967.

Tisdall, Nigel. "Do You Know the Way to San Jose?" *Independent.* February 2, 1996.

"Tribal Rock." *Newsweek.* December 8, 1969.

Vaizey, Marina, "A Wall That Lets You In: Christo and the Running Fence." *The New Republic.* October 23, 1976.

"Violence in America—Getting Worse?" *U.S. News and World Report.* December 11, 1978.

Wolmuth, Roger. "Flower Power Revisited." *People.* June 22, 1987.

OTHER MEDIA

California and the Dream Seekers (Television Miniseries). A&E Television, 1997.

Koch, Chris, and Daniel Zwerdling. "Summer of Love." Weekend All Things Considered. National Public Radio. August 3, 1997.

Secrets of Alcatraz (Television Documentary). The Discovery Channel, 1996.

The Museum of the City of San Francisco website: http://www.sfmuseum.org/hist1/.

INDEX

A

advertisements, Super Bowl 108, 109
Alcatraz 102–5
Alta California 13, 14
Altair 106
Altimira, José 35
Alvarado, Governor 3
American River 21, 24
Anchor Brewery 94–97
Anchorage (AK) 83
Anheuser-Busch Brewery 95
Anthropology Museum of the University of California 67
Apple Computer 109
Apple I 108
Apple II 108
Apple Watch 109
Arguelles, Jose 119, 120
Argüello, José Darío 9, 10
Argüello, Luís Antonio 9
Arguello y Moraga, María de la Concepcíon 10–12
Aspen (CO) 88
August Complex Fire, The, 145

B

Baez, Joan 116
Bates Tavern 42
Baum, Alan 107
Bay Bridge 123, 124
Bear Valley (CA) 42
Bear Flag Revolt 16
Benecia (CA) 23
Benton, Thomas Hart 39, 40
Berkeley (CA) 103
Bodega Bay 11
Bodega Bay (CA) 91–93
Boettcher, Diane 118, 119
Boulder (CO) 119
Brannan, Sam 24
Buena Vista Vinicultural Society 37
Buena Vista Winery 36, 38
Burns, William 28
Byte Shop 108

C

Cabrillo, Juan Rodríguez 1, 2, 3, 4, 5
Canby, General 56, 57
Candlestick Park 122, 123, 124
Candlestick Point (CA) 121

INDEX

Captain Jack 54–57
Caruso, Enrico 61, 62, 64, 65
Castro, Colonel José 14
Central Park (NY) 119
Childs, John C. 79, 81
Christo 110–13
Civil War, The 32, 47, 76
Clear Lake 104
Coloma (CA) 23
Compromise of 1850 80
computer industry 106
Copertini, Cyr 114
coronavirus pandemic, 145
Cortés, Hernando 3
Crescento City (CA) 81
Curly Haired Doctor 54, 56
Curry County (OR) 80
Cushing, Alexander Cochrane 87, 88, 89, 90
Cuyler's Harbor 3
Cypress Street Viaduct 123

D

Del Norte County (CA) 80, 81, 82
DiMaggio, Joe 123
Disney, Walt 89–90
Donner Party 20
Drake's Bay 4

E

Ellis Island (NY) 104
Emperor Francis Joseph of Austria 73
Emperor Norton 51–53
Eureka (CA) 46
Exclusionary Act 59

F

Farish, John B. 62
Feinstein, Dianne 116
Ferrelo, Bartolomé 4, 5

First Marine Division of the United States Army 87
Fong Ching 58, 60
Fort Humboldt 30, 31
Fort Lawton (WA) 104
Fort Ross 4, 11, 21
Fort Vancouver 31
Fox, Douglass 41
Frémont, Jessie Benton 14, 39–43
Frémont, John C. 14, 39, 40, 41, 43
Frémont, Lily 41, 42, 43
French Gordon 106, 107

G

Gable, Gilbert 80, 81
Gage, Tom 124
Gammons, Peter 121
García, Manuel. *See* Three Finger Jack
Genoa (NV) 33
German Kaiser 53
Golden Gate Bridge 60, 90
Golden Gate Park 64, 65, 99
Gold Rush 24, 71, 79, 80
Gooch, Dr. William 120
Grant, Ulysses S. 32
Great Basin, the 17
Great Depression 80
Great Serpent Mound (OH) 119
Great Pyramids 119
Guatemala 3

H

Haight-Ashbury 98, 99, 100
Hale, Prentis 89
Haraszthy, Count Agoston 35–37, 38
Hawaii, John Sutter and 21
Hayden Planetarium 120
Hertz, Alfred 61, 62
Hewlett Packard 106, 107
Highland Hospital 124

INDEX

Hitchcock, Alfred 92
Homebrew Computer Club 106–9
Hornitos 41–43
House of Happy Walls 73
Humboldt Bay 44, 45
Humboldt County 45

I

Ide, William B. 13
Indian Island 42, 43, 44
Innsbruck, Austria 88
International Olympic Committee
  88, 89
Ipad 109
Ipod 109
Ishi (last Yahi Indian) 66–69
Issei 83, 84–86
Isthmus of Panama 30–31

J

Jackson County (OR) 80
Javacheff, Christo. *See* Christo
Jefferson, state of 79–82
Jobs, Steve 107–8
Josephine County (OR) 80
Josephine Mine 41, 13

K

Karok tribe 45
Kibei 85–86
Kientpoos. *See* Captain Jack
Klamath County (CA) 80
Klamath tribe 75, 55
Klondike Gold Rush 71

L

La Porte (CA) 34
Lake Ontario 30
Lake Placid (NY) 88
Lassen County (CA) 80
Leary, Timothy 99

Lincoln, Mary Todd 76
Lincoln, President Abraham 53
Loire Valley 36
London, Charmian 70
London, Jack 70–73
Los Angeles (CA) 36

M

Macbook 109
Machu Picchu 110
Macintosh 109
Manhattan Island (NY) 103
Manzanar (CA) 84
Marin County 110, 111
Mariposas Ranch 40
Marshall, James 16, 21–24
Maurier, Daphne du 93
Maytag, Fritz 94–97
Mendoza, Viceroy 3
Metropolitan Opera of New York
  61
Mexican-American War 26–27
Mexican War 30, 31
Mexico 2, 3, 5
microprocessors 108
Milk, Harvey 114–17
Miller Brewery 95
Mission San Francisco Solano 35
Modoc County (CA) 82
Modoc tribe 45, 54, 55, 56, 57
Moisseiff, Leon, 91
Monterey (CA) 14, 16, 23
Monterey Bay 4
Moore, Fred 106, 107
Moscone, George 114–17
Mount Diablo 23
Mount Shasta 118–20
Mount Shasta City (CA) 109
Murieta, Joaquin 26–29
Murieta, Rosita 27, 28
Murphy, Senator George 103

INDEX

N

Nantucket (MA) 48
Narváez, Pánfilo de 3
Navidad, Mexico 2, 5
New Haven (CT) 75
New Helvetia 20, 21
Newsom, Governor Gavin, 146
Niagara Falls (NY) 119
Nimitz Freeway 123, 124
1984 108–9
1989 World Series 121
1956 Winter Olympics 88
1906 Olympic Games 87
Nisei 84–86
Norton, Joshua Abraham. *See* Emperor
　Norton
Nothemburg, Deputy Mayor Rudy
　104

O

Oakes, Richard 102, 105
Oakes, Yvonne 102
Oakland A's 121, 122
Olympics 87–90
Omnibus Railroad Company 47
Oregon Territory 14, 31
Oregon Trail 55
Oroville (CA) 66, 67

P

Paradise (CA), 146
Patty Reed 17–20
Pearl Harbor (HI) 82, 83
Penutian Family, the 6
personal computers 106, 107
Petaluma (CA) 110
Philadelphia (PA) 48
Placerville (CA) 33, 34
Pleasant, John James 49
Pleasant, Mammy. *See* Pleasant, Mary
　Ellen

Pleasant, Mary Ellen 47–50
Point Concepcíon 2, 4
Polk, President James K. 16, 24
Port Orford (OR) 80
Poulson, Wayne 88, 89
Pozzi, Ed 113
Presidio, the 9, 10, 11, 64
Prohibition 95
Promontory Summit 37

Q

Queen Victoria 53

R

Rattlesnake Island (CA) 104
Reagan, Ronald 100
Reed, Patty 18, 19, 20
Reed, Tommy 18, 19, 20
Reed, Virginia 18
Republic of Texas 15
Rezanov, Nikolai Petrovich 9–12
Rhine Valley 36
Rhône Valley 36
Riffle Gap (CO) 111
Rocky Mountains 14
Rogue River 5
Roosevelt, President Franklin 83
Roosevelt, Theodore 64

S

Sackets Harbor (NY) 30
Sacramento (CA) 16, 25, 37, 41, 53
Sacramento River 22
San Francisco (CA) 4, 14, 24, 31, 50,
　51, 52
　Chinatown and 58–89
　earthquake of 1906 and 62–63
　Ishi and 67, 69
　Marina District and 122, 123
　persecution of Chinese and 60
San Francisco Bay 9, 51, 53

INDEX

San Francisco General Hospital 124
San Francisco Giants 121–22, 124
San Francisco–Oakland Bay Bridge 53
San Jose (CA) 24, 74
San Miguel Island 2, 3, 4
Santa Cruz (CA) 93
secession, from California, 79–82
Sierra Nevada 17
Silicon Valley 106
Sloat, Commander John C. 16
Smith, James Henry 49
Snow Bowl (Reno, NV) 88
Sonoma (CA) 13, 14, 15, 16
Sonoma County 110, 111, 112
Sonoma Valley 35, 36, 37
Sonoma Wine Company 63
Sonora, Mexico 27
South Fork of the American River 21
Squaw Peak 89
Squaw Valley (CA) 87–90
state of Jefferson 79–82
Stockton (CA) 26, 28, 29
Stonehenge 119
Stuyvesant, Peter 103
Sullivan, Fire Chief 64
Summer of Love 98–101
Super Bowl advertisements 108, 109
Sutter, John 12, 24–25
Sutter's Fort 21, 22, 23, 24

T

Tehama County (CA) 82
Terry, Chief Justice 41
Thompson, "Snowshoe" 33–34
Three Finger Jack 27, 28
Todd, William 13, 15
Trinity County (CA) 80
Truckee Lake 17, 20

Tsar of all Russias 53
Tulare Lake 28
Tule Lake (CA) 83, 84, 85, 86

U

Underground Railroad 49
Union Pacific Railroad 52
Uniontown (CA). See Arcata (CA)
University of California at Berkeley 71, 99, 100
U.S. Olympic Committee 88

V

Vallejo, General Mariano 14, 15
Valley Ford (CA) 113
Valley of the Moon Ranch 70, 72, 73
Vincent, Fay 124

W

Waterman, Professor T. T. 67
Webber, Sheriff J. B. 66
Welch, Bob 122, 123
West Point (NY) 30
White, Dan 115–17
White House 76
Winchester, Sarah (Pardee) 74–78
Winchester, William Wirt 75
Winchester Mystery House 74–78
Wintun tribe 6–8
Wiyot tribe 44, 45
Wolf House 70–71, 72
Woodstock (NY) 119
World War II 82
Wozniak, Steve 107, 108

Y

Yahi tribe 67, 68
Yana tribe 68
Yreka (CA) 79, 81

ABOUT THE AUTHOR

Erin H. Turner is a writer and editor living in Helena, Montana. She has a degree in history and gender and women's studies from Grinnell College in Iowa and has traveled extensively throughout the West.